BABY NAMES 2012

Eleanor Turner

white
LADDER

Acknowledgements

I would like to extend my utmost gratitude to Cerys Owen, Shelley Heck, Michael Turner and Robin Boothroyd for their contributions; without them this book would have been much shorter. My thanks are also given to Beth Bishop at Crimson Publishing for her patience and guidance throughout the project. Finally, the greatest thanks go to Owen Henri Turner, who grew patiently inside me while I wrote this book and waited to be born until I had chosen his name.

This third edition published in Great Britain 2011 by
Crimson Publishing, a division of Crimson Business Ltd
Westminster House
Kew Road
Richmond
Surrey
TW9 2ND

First and second editions published by Crimson Publishing in 2009 and 2010.

© Crimson Publishing, 2011

The right of Eleanor Turner to be identified as the author of this work has been asserted by her in accordance with the Copyright, Designs and Patents Act, 1988.

A catalogue record for this book is available from the British Library.

ISBN 978 1 90541 092 7

Typeset by IDSUK (DataConnection) Ltd
Printed and bound by L.E.G.O. S.p.A, Lavis TN

Contents

A note on how to use this book

While the author and publisher acknowledge that baby names vary widely in spelling and pronunciation, this book lists each name only once: under the most common initial and spelling. If a name has an alternative spelling with a different initial, it may be listed under that letter also.

Introduction

Picking a name for your baby is one of the most enjoyable activities for a new parent, but it's also one of the most daunting. Sometimes choosing the right name is simply a case of hearing one you like and knowing instantly that you've chosen correctly. But, for the vast majority of parents the naming game gets far more complicated when you start trying to please parents, grandparents, friends and siblings, while trying to avoid names that could be shortened into ridiculous nicknames or would make for funny initials.

You'll also probably want to choose something unique, but not *too* unique, or something common, but not *too* common. A name could be inspired by an admired celebrity, a sports star, or an influential historical or political figure. It could also come from the family tree, or follow a current baby-naming trend. You also need to make sure you love it – you'll have to live with it forever! The possibilities are endless so it's understandable that it can set some parents into panic mode.

Well, never fear. *Baby Names 2012* is here to take you through your options and solve your baby-naming dilemmas. It's updated annually, so always includes the year's most popular names, celebrity choices, and names making a comeback. We've included dozens of lists to provide you with inspiration, and, of course, some downright weird names children have been given over the years (usually by celebs).

Take a peek at the most up-to-date trends in baby-naming, from the brand new name at the top of the boy's charts after 14 years of Jack to recent celebrity trends. Read about how the Royal Family will influence trends in 2012 (with the Queen's Diamond Jubilee this summer) and what names make for the cleverest kids …

Be sure to also keep an eye out for all the facts and figures we've got for you – including what names are most popular around the world – so you can either go with the flow … or deliberately against it.

The average length of a baby name is six letters.

This book is broken into two sections: the first deals with how to figure out what to name your child through a series of questions and suggestions, and the second gives you a meaning for each name you're considering using. There's no right or wrong way to use this book, just as there's no right or wrong way to make your baby-naming decision.

Remember, picking a baby name should be fun – so dip in, find some names you like and use the suggestions we've given you to work out if one of them is a winner!

part one

1

What was hot in 2011?

Jack fell down and lost his crown

In 2011 the most popular name for baby boys for the past 14 years, Jack, made headlines again. But it wasn't because it topped the charts, it was because the name Oliver had stormed into the top spot and broken Jack's stronghold. This means that the top boy and girl names are now very similar – Oliver and Olivia. The fastest climbers were Maisie for girls (up 29 places to position 34) and Austin for boys (finally reaching the Top 100 after a massive leap of 60 places), while the names Alisha, Keira, Lucas and Brandon all fell out of favour and dropped by at least 10 places each.

Last year was also particularly remarkable because there were no new entries into the Top 10 names for either boys or girls, although there was some jostling for position within the ranks. There were also only six new names in the Top 100 boys' names (Aiden, Arthur, Austin, Frederick, Jude, and Stanley), and a mere three newcomers in the girls' list (Heidi, Mya, and Sara). This is substantially different to past years, where we've seen more than 20 new names in the Top 100.

So, what baby names were popular last year?

Top 10 baby names

Boys	Girls
1. Oliver	1. Olivia
2. Jack	2. Ruby
3. Harry	3. Chloe
4. Alfie	4. Emily
5. Joshua	5. Sophie
6. Thomas	6. Jessica
7. Charlie	7. Grace
8. William	8. Lily
9. James	9. Amelia
10. Daniel	10. Evie

" All British people have plain names, and that works pretty well over there.

Paris Hilton

"

The rise of quirky names continues ...

Since the turn of the millennium an interesting phenomenon has taken place: only 50% of babies born in the UK have had their names represented in the Top 50 baby names list. This means that 50% of all British babies have been given such unique and diverse names that they are not common enough to get listed on the national rankings. This includes variations in spellings too, as the Office for National Statistics uses the exact spelling listed on a birth certificate for its calculations. So, if one child is called Lily (ranked eighth in 2011), and another is called Lilly (ranked 45th), they will still be ranked separately to their classmates Lili and Lillie (neither of which ranked in the Top 100).

One explanation for this is that parents have started to give their child a name *more* unusual than their own. A parent who has enjoyed their slightly unusual name will feel more confident about giving their offspring an even more unique name. If this trend continues into 2012 and beyond, you can be sure that names will get stranger and stranger ...

" Each generation wants new symbols, new people, new names. They want to divorce themselves from their predecessors. "

Jim Morrison

Some of Britain's quirky baby names during the last year have included Paprica, Caramel and Skylark for a girl, and Rocky, Rivers and Red for boys.

2011's fastest-climbing names

Boys	Girls
Aiden	Evie
Arthur	Heidi
Austin	Lexie
Frederick	Maisie
Jude	Mya
Lucas	Sara
Stanley	Sophie

... but traditional names also continue to impress

The Top 10 for both boys and girls has been made up of the same names for the last five years. It seems that although some parents like to be adventurous in their choice of name, many pick one for their child that doesn't have any quirky or weird connotations, avoiding any possible assumptions people may make about an unusual name.

Names such as Alfie, Arthur, Evie, Harry and Heidi had dropped out of mainstream use by the 1970s and became vastly unpopular, but in the last few years names ending in -a, -ie, and -y have started to see a resurgence, particularly as a spelling option for parents who like the sound of a traditional name but want to give it a modern twist. Other old-fashioned names, such as Daniel, Lily, Sophie and William have climbed the popularity ranks in the Top 100 lists, joining such stalwarts as Emily, Charlotte and Thomas.

The traditional Muslim name Mohammed has now become so popular in the UK that if all spelling variations were counted as the same name, it would be the most popular name for baby boys in the country. The spelling 'Mohammed' is the most common (ranked 16th in England and Wales last year), followed by 'Muhammad' (ranked 36th) and 'Mohammad' (62nd). In fact, the spelling 'Mohammed' is already the most popular baby boy name in the West Midlands, and the fourth most popular in London.

The seemingly endless popularity of traditional names in the Top 10 may soon lead to a backlash, with parents avoiding picking the same ones as everyone else they know. It's already started to happen with Jack – will Oliver and Olivia be next?

Colin Firth doesn't like his name, apparently. In 2011 he was quoted as saying: 'Colin is the sort of name you'd give your goldfish for a joke. I once saw an episode of *Blackadder* with a dachshund in it called Colin. It seemed his name alone was supposed to reduce you to fits of laughter.'

The cult of celebrity

As always, the celebrity world continued to dominate choices made by parents in 2011 – but we saw a distinct return to more traditional names.

The name Max is massively popular with celebrities at the moment. It increased in popularity after the birth of Christina Aguilera's son in 2008, and both Jennifer Lopez and Charlie Sheen used it as a name for their twins: Max and Emme were born to JLo and Marc Anthony in 2009, and Charlie Sheen's baby boys, Max and Bob, arrived the same year. Other celebrities have recently followed suit, with Cynthia Nixon and James Cordon both choosing the name Max for their new arrivals in 2011. It was last seen at position 25 in the UK's Top 100 baby boy names, but if celebrities continue to choose it as often as they do, it's only a matter of time before we see it in the Top 10.

Although celebrities are often known for choosing highly original (or simply weird) names for their children, new arrivals in the last year or so have actually been given fairly normal names, and we are starting to see more traditional names gaining popularity with celebs. Variations on the names Olivia (David Tennant's daughter), Thomas (Les Dennis' son), Sophia (Peter Crouch and Abbey Clancey's baby girl), and Zachary (Elton John and David Furnish's new arrival) are all hot picks at the moment. Eva Herzigova and Kym Marsh both chose a name which would not sound out of place in the playground of any school: Philip and Polly, respectively.

Celebrity babies of 2010/2011

Locklyn (Vince Vaughn and Kyla Weber, Dec 2010)
Ever Imre (Alanis Morissette and Mario Treadway,
    Dec 2010)
Zachary Jackson Levon (Elton John and David Furnish,
    Dec 2010)
Bertie (Patsy Palmer and Richard Merkell, Dec 2010)
Faith Margaret (Nicole Kidman and Keith Urban,
    Jan 2011)
Leo (Penelope Cruz and Javier Bardem, Jan 2011)
Flynn (Orlando Bloom and Miranda Kerr, Jan 2011)
Max Ellington (Cynthia Nixon and Christine
    Marinoni, Feb 2011)
Aiden (Rod Stewart and Penny Lancaster, Feb 2011)
Philip (Eva Herzigova and Gregorio Marsiaj, Mar 2011)
Lyra (Sophie Dahl and Jamie Cullum, Mar 2011)
Max (James Corden and Julia Carey, Mar 2011)
Polly (Kym Marsh and Jamie Lomas, Mar 2011)
Hero Harper (Myleene Klass and Graham Quinn,
    Mar 2011)
Olivia (David Tennant and Georgia Moffett, Mar 2011)
Sophia Ruby (Peter Crouch and Abbey Clancy,
    Apr 2011)
Thomas Christopher (Les and Claire Dennis, Apr 2011)
Belle (Holly Willoughby and Dan Baldwin, Apr 2011)
Tia (Rio and Rebecca Ferdinand, Apr 2011)
Monroe and Moroccan Scott (Mariah Carey and Nick
    Cannon, May 2011)
Bear Blu (Alicia Silverstone and Christopher Jarecki,
    May 2011)

Baby Names 2012

In the US charts, the name Elvis dropped out of the top 1,000 US baby names in 2010, the first year it had not made the list since 1954.

In fact, even the more unusual names on the roll call for 2010/2011 aren't that strange: Locklyn (chosen by Vince Vaughn), Lyra (Sophie Dahl), and Belle (Holly Willoughby), for example. Myleene Klass chose the name Hero Harper for her baby girl, which might conjure a smile, but it's actually a nod to her Filipino heritage: the name Hero, or Hiro, is frequently given to children in East Asian countries. Alicia Silverstone and Alanis Morissette went with unique names that might raise a few eyebrows: Bear Blu and Ever Imre – both little boys, and neither name making the Top 1,000 names over the last 100 years!

Mariah Carey and Nick Cannon's twins followed the trend of the wacky celeb baby names – baby girl Monroe named after Marilyn Monroe, and Moroccan Scott named after the Moroccan Room in his parent's penthouse, where Nick proposed … and Scott is Nick's middle name. Mariah sent fans into a frenzy when she strung her name announcement out for hours, getting her followers on Twitter to guess, with a clue.

After Britney Spears named her second son Jayden James in 2006, the name became the second most popular name for baby boys in New York City.

Crazy celebrity baby names of recent years

Apple (Gwyneth Paltrow and Chris Martin)

Blue Angel (U2's The Edge and Aislinn O'Sullivan)

Bluebell Madonna (Geri Halliwell)

Bronx Mowgli (Ashlee Simpson and Pete Wentz)

Brooklyn (David and Victoria Beckham – also parents to Romeo and Cruz)

Cosima Violet (Claudia Schiffer and Matthew Vaughn)

Dixie Dot (Anna Ryder Richardson)

Egypt Dauode Dean (Alicia Keys and Swizz Beatz)

Ever Imre (Alanis Morissette and Marlo Treadway)

Kal-El (Nicholas Cage; Kal-El is Superman's original birth name)

Buddy Bear Maurice (Jules and Jamie Oliver – also parents to Daisy Boo, Poppy Honey, and Petal Blossom Rainbow)

Shiloh Nouvel (Brad Pitt and Angelina Jolie)

Sparrow (Nicole Richie and Joel Madden – also parents to Harlow)

Sunday Rose (Nicole Kidman and Keith Urban)

Zuma Nesta Rock (Gwen Stefani and Gavin Rossdale)

Tom Cruise and Katie Holmes learnt a lesson about the woes of celebrity naming, when they found out their daughter Suri's name meant 'from Syria' and not 'princess' in Hebrew, as they'd thought.

Baby Names 2012

The impact of characters in TV shows, movies, and books has been having a huge impact on baby names in the last few years, with the name Isabella jumping up 42 positions since 1999 thanks to Stephanie Meyer's *Twilight* series, and the character of Quinn in *Glee* responsible for more baby boys *and* girls having the same name.

An Israeli couple have called their baby girl 'Like' after the Facebook button. Their other children are called Pie and Vash, which means honey.

14

2

What does 2012 hold for baby names?

Will these trends continue?

Looking forward to 2012, the trend for choosing either old-fashioned or very unique names for babies seems set to continue.

One interesting development in 2012 might be the increase in the number of children given royal names. After the massive popularity of the 2011 weddings of Prince William and Kate Middleton, and Zara Phillips and Mike Tindall, and also the Queen's Diamond Jubilee in this year, the Royal Family has never been so accessible. As well as names such as Willliam, Catherine, Elizabeth, and Philip, we may see other regal names start to appear: think Diana, Victoria,

15

Edward, and Henry. Even Grace Kelly (who married Prince Rainier of Monaco in 1956) could see her names appear on birth certificates everywhere, after the comparisons made between her and Kate's wedding dresses.

It seems likely that parents will continue the recent trend of naming their children shortened versions of longer, more traditional names. The name Maisie, for example, is a shortened version of Margaret, while Bobby is more usually known as Robert.

Predicted 2012 Top 10 baby names

Boys	Girls
1. Oliver	1. Olivia
2. Jack	2. Chloe
3. Harry	3. Ruby
4. Alfie	4. Sophie
5. Joshua	5. Emily
6. Charlie	6. Jessica
7. William	7. Lily
8. Thomas	8. Amelia
9. James	9. Grace
10. George	10. Evie

2012 events

Other influences on the names parents choose in 2012 may come from the worlds of sport, politics, and celebrity.

The Summer Olympics and Paralympics will be hosted in 2012 by the city of London. It stands to reason that the heroes of these games will inspire some parents to name their children after them; past Olympic winners for Great Britain have included Steve Redgrave, Kelly Holmes and Amir Khan, and, as these three athletes will be mentoring 2012 contenders, it's possible that their success will be reflected in baby names statistics. Keep an eye out for babies called Paula (Radcliffe), Jessica (Ennis), and Phillips (Idowu), and also the names of any medal winners.

The eyes of football fans in the UK will be resting on the outcome of the first entry by a team from Great Britain into the Olympic football competition since 1960. While there is still some indecisiveness about who will actually make up the men's and women's teams, it will be interesting to see who will become important players during these crucial matches. Also taking place in 2012 is the UEFA EURO 2012, hosted this time in Poland and Ukraine. Successful football stars often have babies named after them, with names such as Wayne (Rooney), Thierry (Henry) and Ryan (Giggs) all peaking in popularity during large sporting events. Up-and-coming British stars include Jack Wilshire, Scott Parker and Aaron Lennon. Watch out for their names jumping up the chart.

2012 will see an important political battle take place in the USA in November: the presidential election. You can be sure that the election will be closely observed by the media on both sides of the pond. However, it's not true to say that children are frequently named after presidents or prime ministers; President Barack Obama's name has yet to enter even the Top 1,000 in the USA, and David Cameron's first name has dropped 22 places in the last 10 years. Interestingly though, there is a trend of naming babies after the *children* of politicians – Barack Obama's daughters are named Maliyah and Sasha, and a variation of both of these appear in the USA's Top 100 names for girls. When David Cameron's newborn daughter was named Florence in 2010, the media went wild, and a flurry of parents started choosing this name for their baby girls shortly after. It is expected to enter the UK's Top 100 for the first time in 2012.

Don't forget to register your baby's birth! Labour leader Ed Miliband came under scrutiny when he didn't register his first son's birth in 2009. As he and his partner, Justine Thornton, weren't then married, Miliband was supposed to attend the registration with her so he could be listed as the baby's father, but neglected to do so. (He was present at the registration of his second son's birth in November 2010).

2012 anniversaries

Significant anniversaries can potentially influence baby names. In 2012 this includes the 200th anniversary of the War of 1812, the 100th anniversary of the sinking of the Titanic, 100 years since the first list of birthstones was released by the Jewelers of America association, and the Queen's Diamond Jubilee – meaning she has been on the throne for 60 years. It will also be Charles Dickens' 200th birthday, 150 years since the birth of composer Claude Debussy, and 100 years since mathematician Alan Turing was born.

Remarkably, 2012 will see the 50th anniversary of the James Bond 007 series of films. *Dr. No*, the film which shot star Sean Connery to fame, was first released in 1962, and the anniversary coincides with the release of the yet-to-be-named Bond 23 in November, starring Daniel Craig. Martini, anyone?

Celebrating their first wedding anniversary, but 11 years since they first met, will be Prince William and his wife Catherine. After all the majesty and ceremony during their wedding in 2011, it will be interesting to see how they, and the media, report back on their first year of marriage – particularly if they have started a family.

Of course, the year 2012 cannot be discussed without some mention of the significance of the Mayan Calendar, which ends on 21 December 2012 and supposedly symbolises the end of days. However you interpret the theories and mystery surrounding the Mayan Calendar, you can be sure it will be mentioned heavily in the months preceding December.

Don't be surprised, therefore, if the names Charles, Claude, Rose and Jack (from the movie *Titanic*), Elizabeth, William, Kate, Maya, and even some names of birthstones all jump in popularity in 2012. The very fact these names will be brought to the nation's attention by the media will mean parents will start to consider them as potential candidates, even if they would never have considered them previously.

2012 anniversary names

Boys	Girls
Alan	Catherine
Charles	Diamond
Claude	Elizabeth
Daniel	Garnet
Jack	Kate
James	Maya
Philip	Pearl
Roger	Rose
Sean	Ruby
William	Sapphire

The influence of pop culture

Pop culture will be perhaps the most prominent influence on baby names in the coming year. Celebrity couples expecting babies in late 2011 and 2012 include Jessica Alba and Cash Warren, Mel B and Stephen Belafonte, Kate Hudson, and Jodie Kidd. If the choices of names these celebrities make are particularly noteworthy, they may well influence the choices made by the general population.

> Words have meaning and names have power
> Anoymous

Expected new arrivals in 2011/2012

Emma Bunton and Jade Jones	(May 2011)
David Schwimmer and Zoe Buckman	(May 2011)
Pink and Carey Hart	(Spring 2011)
Natalie Portman and Benjamin Millepied	(Spring 2011)
Jennifer Connolley and Paul Bettany	(June 2011)
Selma Blair and Jason Bleick	(July 2011)
Victoria and David Beckham	(July 2011)
Kate Hudson and Matt Bellamy	(Summer 2011)
Mel B and Stephen Belafonte	(Summer 2011)
Jessica Alba and Cash Warren	(Autumn 2011)
Jodie Kidd and Andrea Vianini	(Autumn 2011)
Kimberley Stewart and Benicio Del Toro	(Autumn 2011)
Guy Ritchie and Jacqui Ainsely	(Autumn 2011)
Johnny Knoxville and Naomi Nelson	(Autumn 2011)
Alex and Steven Gerrard	(Autumn 2011)
Carla Bruni-Sarkozy and Nicholas Sarkozy	(Autumn 2011)

The release of the eighth and final Harry Potter movie closed a chapter on the impressive climb to fame for the names Harry, Hermione, Ronald, and Ginny, and it seems likely that these names will no longer appear in the Top 100 from 2012 onwards (with the exception of Harry, which has stayed in the Top 10 since 2000). However, the James Bond 007 dynasty, which has grossed more than the Harry Potter series overall, is expected to reignite interest in the names James (Bond), Daniel (Craig), and even Judi (Dench), when the 23rd installment is released.

The movie version of J.R.R. Tolkien's classic book *The Hobbit* is on schedule to hit movie theatres in 2012, and if the influence of the *Lord of the Rings* flicks are anything to go by, *The Hobbit* will also be huge (no pun intended!). Of course you won't see many children named Bilbo Baggins come 2013, but there may be a few little girls named Saoirse or little boys named Elijah, after the actors Saoirse Ronan and Elijah Wood. Even Martin Freeman, who will be playing the part of Bilbo Baggins, might see his name appearing more frequently – although the last time it was in the Top 100 was more than a decade ago.

Other movies set to be released in 2012 include *Men in Black 3*, *Bourne Legacy*, *Breaking Dawn – Part 2*, and *Life of Pi*. At the time of printing there is also speculation that a widely anticipated new TV series about the end of the world according to the Mayan Calendar, called *2012*, will be hitting the small screen, and is set to become as addictive as *Lost*. Watch out for the names of characters from these shows, or the actors playing those characters, to suddenly become immensely popular!

If you need inspiration, why not try following the latest trend from the USA and consider a character from your favourite book or film? The names Edward, Isabella, and Jacob have all leapt in popularity since the release of

Twilight by Stephanie Meyer, and Isabella now tops the charts for baby girls. Even surnames of these characters have increased in popularity: the name Cullen jumped 300 places in a single year.

Popular TV programmes set to air in 2012 include the third series of Miranda Hart's self-titled comedy show, the return of the barrister-based drama series *Silk*, and another series of the recently returned, *Upstairs Downstairs*. Actors Jean Marsh, Ed Stoppard, Claire Foy, and Art Malik play characters with such wonderfully imaginative names as Rose Buck, Sir Hallam Holland, Lady Persephone Towyn, and Amanjit Singh, and fans of the series – both old and new – might pick up a few ideas for baby names as they watch the drama unfold.

Rising stars

Boys	Girls
Amanjit	Bella
Daniel	Isabella
Edward	Judi
Elijah	Maya
Hallam	Miranda
Harry	Persephone
James	Quinn
Martin	Rose
Quinn	Saoirse

3

How to choose a name

Top tips on choosing a name

- **Fall in love with the name(s) you've chosen.** If you plough through hundreds of names in this book and none of them jump off the page at you, then you probably haven't found the right one yet. Likewise, if a relative, friend, or even your spouse suggests a name and you wrinkle your nose every time you hear it, it's not the name for your baby. You should pick a name that you can shout with confidence across the schoolyard, or hear with pride when they graduate from university. Pick a name that makes you smile because if you love it, hopefully your child will too.

- **Don't listen to other people.** Sometimes, grandparents and friends will offer 'advice' during this time which may not always be welcome. This is worth bearing in mind if you've fallen in love with a name and it's either slightly unusual or doesn't follow the set pattern your partner's family have used for the last 50 years. Sharing your choice of name with other people can lead them to criticise it, which you'd probably rather not hear if you've got your heart set on it. Also, if you're bucking with tradition and don't plan on calling your newborn after their great-great-great-grandfather, keeping it a secret until after the birth and registration can work to your advantage. Trust your own instincts and remember: no-one will really care once they see your baby. Its name will simply be its name.

- **Find a name with meaning.** When my parents discovered they were expecting a baby, they sought out possibilities that *meant* something. Both interested in history, they eventually settled on naming their three daughters after Queens of England (Alexandra, Eleanor and Victoria), hoping to fill their children's souls with a sense of pride and importance. It worked, because throughout our lives we have all felt a duty to do our names justice in the modern world. Having a name that has a back story helps your child understand their significance in the world, so whether you name them after a religious saint or prophet, an important political figure or a hero in a Greek tragedy, ensure they know where their name came from. They may just be inspired to be as great as their namesake.

- **Have fun.** Picking out names should be a fun process. Laughing at the ones you'd never dream of choosing can really help you narrow it down to the ones you would. You can also experiment with different spellings, pronunciations or variations of names you like, or go to places where you might feel inspired. Some of the best names come from the worlds of nature and literature, so why not go down to your local garden centre or library and have fun with the classic, cute and downright silly words you find there?

- **Expand your mind.** Don't rule out the weird ones just yet! As a teenager I went to school with a girl named Siam. Her parents had conceived her on a honeymoon trip to Thailand and given her the country's old name as a result. She loved growing up and having an unusual name, as I'm sure Brooklyn Beckham (Posh and Becks's son) and Bronx Wentz (Ashley Simpson and Pete Wentz's son) do too. Also, don't be afraid to play around with spellings and pronunciations, even if the results are a little less than conformist. The name Madison, for example, could be spelt Maddison, Madyson, Maddiesun or even Maddeesunn if you so choose, although you might want to be careful you don't saddle your child with an impossible name to spell, pronounce *and* fit onto a passport application form.

- **Try it out.** While you're pregnant, talk to your baby and address it using a variety of your favourite names to see if it responds. There are numerous stories of names being chosen because the baby kicked when it was called Charlie or Aisha, but was suspiciously silent when it was

called Dexter or Mildred, so see if it has a preference!
You can also try writing names down and sticking them
to your fridge, or saying one out loud enough times to
see if you ever get sick of it. That name you picked out
when you were eight and always said you'd name your
first child, for example, might not sound so appropriate
now you're an adult and have to name a human being
for real.

- **What if you can't agree?** This is probably the trickiest
problem in the baby-naming process to solve. It's wise
to research a number of names you and your partner
are both interested in and make a point of discussing
your reasons for liking or disliking them long before the
baby is due to be born. The labour and delivery room
is probably not the best time to argue as you'll both be
tired, emotional and at least one of you will be in pain.
Avoid sticking to your guns on a name one of you really
isn't happy with because it might lead to resentment
down the line, with your baby caught in the middle. You
could try compromising and picking two middle names
so you both have a name in there you love, or you could
each have five names you're allowed to 'veto' but no
more. You could also try making contractions out of
names you both like, such as Anna and Lisa (Annalisa)
or James and Hayden (Jayden). Whichever way you go
about it, it's important that you eventually agree on the
name you are giving your baby, even if it means losing
out on the one you've had your heart set on for a while.

Think to the future

“ Always end the name of your child with a vowel, so that when you yell the name will carry. ”

Bill Cosby

One important aspect of naming your child is thinking ahead to their future. Will the name you've chosen stand the test of time? Will names popular in 2012 remain popular in 2040? Will they be able to confidently enter a room and give a crucial business presentation with an awkward or unpronounceable name? Will they be able to hand their business card over to a potential client without that client looking bemused every time? Even on a smaller scale, can they survive the potential minefields of primary and secondary school with a name that could be easily shortened to something embarrassing?

While it seems a very long way off now, it is important to think about the impact your chosen name will have on your child's life, and how they will cope with that name as an adult. Introducing themselves as Professor Xavier to a group of university deans might raise a few smirks among knowing *X-Men* fans, as would any unusual or trendy 2012 name which has lost its shine by 2040. Would you want to try catching criminals as Police Officer Apple Blossom or have other politicians take you seriously with a name like MP Lil' Kim Scarlett? You don't want to give your child a name which they just cannot live with for the rest of their lives, so make your choice based on what's appropriate for a child as well as an adult. To make this easier you might want to choose a longer name which can be shortened or extended as your child desires.

Banned names

The following names were all banned by registration officials in New Zealand:

- Cinderella Beauty Blossom
- Fat Boy
- Fish and Chips (twins)
- Keenan Got Lucy
- O.crnia
- Sex Fruit
- Stallion
- Talula Does The Hula From Hawaii
- Twisty Poi
- Yeah Detroit

This was because New Zealand law prevents parents from giving their children names which would cause offence or are more than 100 characters long.

Allowed names

These names, however, were all permitted by the same officials:

- All Blacks
- Benson and Hedges (twins)
- Ford Mustang
- Kaos

Masport and Mower (twins)
Midnight Chardonnay
Number 16 Bus Shelter
Spiral Cicada
Superman (changed from 4real)
Violence

Stereotypes – true or false?

Will the name you choose actually affect your child's life?
Will names that seem clever make your child brainier?
Will names with positive meanings make your child into a
happier person? The answer is … possibly.

Some experts believe that parents who choose inspirational
names for their offspring (Destiny, Serenity, Unique) or
names of products they would like to own (Armani, Jaguar,
Mercedes) are projecting a future onto their child for them
to aspire to, and therefore help shape their child's life.

Inspirational names

Destiny	Joy
Happy	Peace
Heaven	Serenity
Hope	Unique
Innocence	Unity

Future aspirations names

Armani	Ferrari
Aston	Jaguar
Bugatti	Mercedes
Chanel	Porsche
Dolce	Prada

One thing to consider when baby naming is how your child's name will be perceived by the outside world. Typically, judgements are passed on names before a person is met, such as at job interviews or in school. This does have the potential to hold back your child, although there is conflicting evidence to say that once someone is met in person, assumptions and stereotypes are wiped away.

The latest research indicates that there are certain names more likely to initiate strong responses in people than others. A recent study analysed the number of stickers given to children as rewards for good behaviour. Children named Abigail and Jacob are more likely to be praised for being well behaved than children named Beth and Josh, and children who do not shorten their name or go by nicknames are more likely to be better behaved, too.

In 2011 teachers across the country were asked to decide from a list of names which children were more likely to be badly behaved than others. Topping the 'naughty' charts were Callum, Connor, and Jack for boys, and Chelsea, Courtney, and Chardonnay for girls, while the names in the 'clever' category were Alexander, Adam, and Christopher for boys, and Elizabeth, Charlotte, and Emma for girls.

Teachers were also asked to pick names they felt were likely to be given to 'popular' children, and these included Jack, Daniel, and Charlie, and Emma, Charlotte, and Hannah. Meaning little boys named Jack are naughty, but popular!

Teachers in a different survey were asked to pick names they felt were particularly 'chavvy'. Chantelle, Jordan, Kylie, and Paige came out on top for the girls, and Connor, Dwayne, Liam, and Rhys were ranked first for the boys. Around the same time, it was discovered that teenagers named Katharine and Duncan were up to eight times more likely to achieve high GCSE results than those named Wayne or Jermaine.

Names which mean 'clever'

Abner	Shanahan
Cassidy	Todd
Haley	Ulysses
Penelope	Washington
Portia	Wylie

Names which sound 'clever'

Alastair	Gabriel
Charles	Harriet
Christian	Sophia
Elizabeth	Spencer
Frances	William

Children who are told they have inherited an ancestor's name or that of an influential character from history seem to be more driven and focused than children who are told disappointingly, 'we just liked the sound of it'. As a parent, it seems it's okay to pick an unusual name if you have the story or anecdotal evidence to back it up. Naming your child Atticus (after Atticus Finch from Harper Lee's *To Kill A Mockingbird*, known for being a strong and moral character) may therefore not be a bad idea …

However, there is no actual scientific evidence to prove the power of names directly affects someone's life – it's all anecdotal.

Personality and character have a far greater influence than name alone and after a while, a name becomes just a name.

Quirky names

There are lots of disadvantages to having a quirky name, but there are plenty of advantages too. For one thing, your child's name will never be forgotten by other people, and if they do something influential with their life their name could become inspirational for other parents to name their children. On the other hand, a quirky name often requires a quirky personality. If you don't think your genes could stand up to a name like Satchel or Kerensa, perhaps it's time to think of one a little more run-of-the-mill.

It's not true that babies are as influenced by their names as people believe. There is no scientific evidence to say that names dictate who we become, which means that you cannot give your child a perfect or imperfect name, whichever one you finally pick. However, a survey carried out recently by the National Centre for Social Research found that the more unusual the name, the less likely a candidate is to be called for a job interview after submitting a CV. Whether or not this fact would affect a child's development and future career is yet to be determined, but it is something to consider.

While parents are often discouraged from picking wild and crazy names for their babies (think about Zuma Nesta Rock, Gwen Stefani's second son) there isn't actually any evidence to suggest that children are hindered in any way by them, unless they're really, really extreme.

French law prohibits all names other than those on an approved list.

What not to call your child …

In Pennsylvania in December 2008 there was a case of a supermarket bakery refusing to ice the words 'Happy Birthday, Adolf Hitler' onto a three-year-old's birthday cake, despite never having met the child it was intended for. The parents were able to eventually fulfill the order at another shop, but as a result of the publicity surrounding the event Social Services were called in to assess the child's home and Adolf, along with his siblings JoyceLynn Aryan Nation and Honszlynn Hinler Jeannie, were taken into care.

Controversial names adopted by real people

Adolf Hitler

Beelzebub

Desdemona

Hannibal Lecter

Himmler

Jezebel

Lucifer

Mussolini

Stalin

Voldemort

Disease names throughout history

Fever Bender (born 1856)

Leper Priest (born 1929)

Cholera Priest (born 1830)

Rubella Graves (born 1814)

Typhus Black (born 1897)

Hysteria Johnson (born 1881)

Emma Royd (born 1850)

Kathryn E. Coli (born 1894)

Mumps Sykes (born 1891)

Helen Fairey of Derby changed her name by deed poll to Christmas Fairy in 2010. She now works for a large hotel chain, ensuring guests have plenty of Christmas cheer every year.

Nicknames

❝Nicknames stick to people, and the most ridiculous are the most adhesive.
Thomas C. Haliburton **❞**

Nicknames are unavoidable. They can range from the common – Mike from Michael, Sam from Samantha – to the trendy, funny or downright insulting. I've lost count of the number of Richards who refuse to be called 'Dick'.

The first time your child encounters a nickname will probably be before they're even born, or at least within the first few months. Many older siblings find new names hard to remember or pronounce and your baby could end up with a nickname before you know it. If your baby has an older sibling, try talking to them about their new brother or sister using the name you've chosen so you can discover how their imagination might choose to interpret it. If they're an older child you might even want to include them in the naming process from the start, if for no other reason than they mention a friend at school who gets teased for having an unfortunate nickname derived from the name you've chosen.

However, having said this, it is perfectly possible to choose a name that you know has an unfortunate nickname associated with it but for it to not bother you. If you don't encourage the use of nicknames when your child is young, the chances are one won't stick when they're older either. I, for example, don't tell anyone I meet as an adult that I was known as Nell for the better half of my childhood, so no-one calls me that now. Another way to avoid embarrassing nicknames is to select one for your child that you actually like so that others don't even get a mention. Call your daughter Elizabeth by the names Liz, Lizzie or Libby if you don't like Betty or Beth, and no-one will even consider the alternatives.

You can pre-empt problem nicknames to some extent by saying the name you've chosen out loud and trying to find rhymes for it. This is a clever way to avoid playground chants and nursery rhyme-type insults, such as Andy Pandy or Looby Lou. It's a sad truth, though, that children will rhyme anything with anything else if they can, so while you might wish to take playground chants into account during your naming process, don't be too concerned about them. Most children are subjected to it at some point and emerge unscathed.

A Chinese couple were prevented from naming their child '@' in 2007, despite their reasoning that it was simply a modern choice of name in this technological age.

Using family names

Some families have a strong tradition of using names for babies that come from the family tree. There are instances where naming your son Augustine VIII is simply not an option; it's a rule. Another way families do this is to give children the name of their parent of the same sex and add 'Junior' (Jr) to the end. This could potentially create a problem if that child then decides to carry on the tradition and name their child after themselves – after all, who wants to be known as Frederick Jr Jr?

There are pros and cons with using family names:

- Pro: Your child will feel part of a strong tradition, which will create a sense of security for them and help make them feel a complete member of the family.

- Pro: If you're having a problem selecting a name you and your partner both agree on, this is a very simple solution and will make your new child's family very happy.

- Con: You might not actually like the name that's being passed down. Naming your child the 12th Thumbelina in a row might not actually hold the same attraction for you as for the generation before.

- Con: Another drawback could be if the cultural associations with that name have changed in your lifetime and it is no longer appropriate.

One way to navigate around choosing a family name is to compromise. You could use the name as a middle name, or refer to your baby by a nickname instead. You could also suggest using a name from the other partner's family: if the name comes from your side, try finding one you like from the other side. If their argument is for tradition then this is an astonishingly effective counter-argument.

Whatever you decide about using family names, just remember that this is *your* baby. Just as your parents got to decide what they named you, you get to decide this. If family and friends are disappointed, don't be alarmed. Once the baby is here all they will see is how much she has her grandmother's nose or his grandfather's ears, and the name will become far less important.

Traditional names

Boys	Girls
Arthur	Ava
Charlie	Dorothy
Edward	Elizabeth
Fred	Grace
Harry	Louisa
Henry	Margaret
Joseph	Martha
Julian	Mary
Miles	Olivia
William	Rosemary

Top 10 boy's names in 1904 and 1984

1904	1984
1. William	1. Arthur
2. John	2. James
3. George	3. Charles
4. Thomas	4. Frederick
5. Albert	5. Michael

6. Ernest	6. Matthew
7. Christopher	7. Andrew
8. James	8. Richard
9. David	9. Paul
10. Daniel	10. Mark

Top 10 girl's names in 1904 and 1984

1904	**1984**
1. Mary	1. Sarah
2. Florence	2. Laura
3. Doris	3. Gemma
4. Edith	4. Emma
5. Dorothy	5. Rebecca
6. Annie	6. Claire
7. Margaret	7. Victoria
8. Alice	8. Samantha
9. Elizabeth	9. Rachel
10. Elsie	10. Amy

Spellings and pronunciation

Once you've finally agreed upon a name, it's time to think about how you wish it to be spelt and pronounced. Some parents love experimenting with unusual variations of traditional names, while others prefer names to be instantly recognisable. The only advice here is to use caution in your experiments. There are many tales of parents seeing or hearing pretty names in the hospital during delivery and choosing them for their children, only to find out later they were medical terms and therefore completely inappropriate as names. Even spelling or pronouncing them differently won't be of much use once they're old enough to know the meaning behind them.

Actual medical terms used as names

Chlamydia (pronounced cler-mid-EE-ya)
Eczema (pronounced ex-SEE-mah)
Female (pronounced fuh-MAH-lee)
Latrine (pronounced lah-TREE-nee)
Meconium (pronounced meh-COH-nee-um)
Syphilis (pronounced see-PHIL-iss)
Testicles (pronounced TESS-tee-clees)
Urine (pronounced yer-REE-nee)
Vagina (pronounced vaj-EE-nah)

Obviously the examples above are a little extreme, but the choices you make regarding spelling and pronunciation are really important. Try to avoid making a common name too long or too unusual in its spelling as this will be the first thing your child learns how to write. They will also be subjected to constant corrections during their lifetime, as other people misspell or mispronounce their name in ever more frustrating patterns. Make sure the name isn't too long that it won't fit on forms or name badges, as they'll simply stop using it and take on a nickname instead. Substituting the odd 'i' for a 'y' isn't too bad, but turning the name Jonathan into Jonnaythanne doesn't do anyone any favours.

Britain has seen an increase in 'text' language spellings

An	Jaicub
Camron	Jayk
Conna	Lora
Ema	Patryk
Esta	Samiul
Flicity	Summa
Helin	Wilym

Middle names

The use of middle names is pretty standard practice these days. In fact, it has become fairly uncommon to name a child *without* a middle name. A middle name can have just as much of an impact as a forename so your choice for your own baby should be made as carefully as their first name.

You may have already decided what middle name to give your child due to tradition or culture, in which case the following advice may be moot. In Spanish cultures, for example, middle names are often the mother's surname or other name to promote that matriarchal lineage. Similarly, parents who have not taken each other's surnames or are not married may choose to give their child one surname as a middle name and one as a last name so both parents are represented. Other traditions may use an old family name, passed down to each first-born son or daughter to encourage a sense of family pride and history. A decision about what middle name to pass on may have therefore already been made for you, even before your own birth.

The shortest baby names are only two letters long (Al, Ed, Jo and Ty), but the longest could be any length imaginable. Popular 11 letter-long names include Bartholomew, Christopher, Constantine, and Maximillian.

If you are choosing a middle name there are some common trends for 2012 to help you narrow it down.

- **Opposite-length names.** It has become very popular to give a child either a long forename and short middle name, or a short forename and long middle name. If this idea attracts you, consider using syllables to give you an idea of length and combinations.

  - Generally, if the forename has only one or two syllables (Owen, Steven, Yasmin, Zoe) then the middle name should have two, three or even four syllables (Owen Jonathan, Steven Michael, Yasmin Samantha, Zoe Jessica).

  - If the opposite is true and the forename is three or four syllables long (Anthony, Jennifer, Nicholas, Rosemary), the middle name may be better kept to only one or two syllables (Anthony Kevin, Jennifer Ruth, Nicholas John, Rosemary Dawn).

- **Names from the family tree.** Honouring your ancestors is another popular trend for 2012. Parents are frequently looking back to their own lineage for interesting, unusual or influential names.

Mariah Carey and Nick Cannon took two different approaches to middle names with their twins. They gave their baby boy Moroccan the middle name Scott – as it is not only Nick's middle name, but also his grandmother's maiden name – but decided not to give their baby girl Monroe a middle name, as Mariah doesn't have one either.

- **Unusual names.** Along with a wider variety of first names in recent years (Ruby, Amelia, and Mia have all climbed the Top 20 charts over the last few years), parents are choosing more unusual middle names too. This would make sense, as a child named Bronte or Keilyn probably needs a fairly uncommon middle name to balance it out. Alternatively, as middle names are far less frequently used, this is an opportunity for parents to have an unusual name included that they wouldn't perhaps use otherwise. If their child grows up not to like it they have the option of only using their initial, or simply dropping it from daily use altogether.

- **Common names.** As a last resort, if you find you are struggling to choose a middle name you could always pick a traditionally used one. For girls, Grace, Marie, May, and Rose have all been strikingly popular in 2011 and 2012 and the same is true for Christopher, David, Jackson, and Thomas for boys.

It is becoming more and more common to give a parent's first name as a middle name to newborns.

Popular middle names in 2012

Boys	Girls
Adam	Anne
Alexander	Elise
Christopher	Elizabeth
David	Grace
Jackson	Louise
Joseph	Marie
Lee	May
Michael	Nicole
Steven	Rose
Thomas	Ruth

As with first names, middle names can have hilarious consequences if not thought about carefully. It's worth writing down your favourite combinations and saying them out loud to make sure you're not making one of these mistakes …

Amusing middle name combinations

Blanche Kerr Tane (blanche curtain)

Claire May Dye (Claire may die)

Harry Armand Bach (hairy arm and back)

Justin Miles North (just ten miles north)

Laura Lynne Hardy (Laurel and Hardy)

Liz May Read (Liz may read)

Mary Annette Woodin (marionette wooden)

Norma Leigh Lucid (normally lucid)

May Ann Naze (mayonnaise)

Sam Ann Fisher (salmon fisher)

Of course, you don't have to narrow down middle name choices to just one. It is becoming more and more common to have several middle names, particularly if parents like more than one or want to include a family name as well. Be careful not to have too many though, as this makes life very difficult when filling out official forms or enrolling your child in school. Most institutions only recognise one middle name, and some only recognise a middle initial.

Many people actually choose to go by their middle name instead of their forename, so it could be seen as a safety net if you're worried your child won't like their name. In fact, you probably know someone in your family or workplace that has always been known as Ed or Sam when their name is actually James Edward Jones or Felicity Samantha Taylor.

The Glastonbury teenager named **Captain Fantastic Faster Than Superman Spiderman Batman Wolverine Hulk And The Flash Combined**, changed his name from George Garratt in 2008. He claims to have the longest name in the world. If he does then he replaces Texan woman **Rhoshandiatellyneshiaunneveshenk Koyaanisquatsiuth Williams**, whose 57-letter length name pales in comparison to Captain's 81.

Celebrities who go by middle names

Antonio Banderas (Jose Antonio Dominguez Banderas)
Bob Marley (Nesta Robert Marley)
Dakota Fanning (Hannah Dakota Fanning)
Will Ferrell (John William Ferrell)
Kelsey Grammar (Allen Kelsey Grammar)
Ashton Kutcher (Christopher Ashton Kutcher)
Hugh Laurie (James Hugh Calum Laurie)
Evangeline Lilly (Nicole Evangeline Lilly)
Brad Pitt (William Bradley Pitt)
Brooke Shields (Christa Brooke Camille Shields)
Reese Witherspoon (Laura Jean Reese Witherspoon)

Initials

What surname will your baby have? Does its first letter lend itself easily to amusing acronyms already, and would choosing certain forenames only exacerbate the problem?

If your child will inherit a double-barrelled surname this becomes a bigger consideration still, as there are more amusing four letter words than there are three. My brother-in-law was going to be called Andrew Steven Schmitt before he was born, until his parents realised at the last minute what his initials would spell ...

It's worth taking the time to think about acronyms of initials in the real world too, such as how names are displayed on credit cards or imagining your child's name written out on a form. Nobody should have to go through life known as S. Lugg because their parents didn't think that far ahead.

Amusing initials

Earl E. Bird	S. Lugg
Kay F. Cee	Warren T.
I. P. Freely	I.C. Blood
Al E. Gador	H. I. Vee
Angie O. Graham	Gene E. Yuss

> **I call everyone 'darling' because I can't remember their names.**
>
> Zsazsa Gabor

Amusing acronyms of real people

Samuel Alan Spencer – SAS

Sally Theresa Donaghue – STD

Neil Christopher Parker – NCP (the car park)

James John Brookes – JJB (the sportswear shop)

Jake Clive Baxter – JCB

Patricia Mary Simpson – PMS

David Vernon Durante – DVD

Victoria Helen Smith – VHS

Jennifer Paige Garrett – JPG

George Barry Holmes – GBH

Across the UK, there are people whose initials spell out three letter words – from RAT and FAG to FAB or POP – and some are better than others, so do check!

Your surname

Tied to your child's potential new initials is their new surname. Whether they are receiving their name from their mother, father or a hyphenated combination of both, matching an appropriate first name to their surname is an important undertaking. Try to avoid forenames that might lead to unfortunate outcomes if they get combined with certain surnames, to prevent a lifetime of embarrassment for your baby. The best way to work out if this might happen is to write down all the names you like alongside your child's last name and have someone else read them out loud. This second pair of eyes and ears might just spot something you didn't.

Unfortunate first name/surname combinations

Anna Sasin

Barb Dwyer

Barry Cade

Ben Dover

Duane Pipe

Grace Land

Harry Rump

Hazel Nutt

Isabella Horn

Jenny Taylor

Justin Time

Mary Christmas

Oliver Sutton

Paige Turner

Russell Sprout

Stan Still

Teresa Green

There is also the danger of your child being subjected to having a spoonerism made out of their name, where the first letters or syllables get swapped around to form new words. Named after the Reverend Dr William Archibald Spooner (1844–1930), a spoonerism can be created out of almost anything to make clever, amusing, or downright inappropriate phrases instead. An unfortunate and recent example of this would be Angelina Jolie and Brad Pitt's daughter Shiloh, whom they named Shiloh Jolie-Pitt to avoid the inevitable Shiloh Pitt spoonerism. Try to avoid making the same mistake!

The micro-blogging site Twitter has recently become a hot spot for spoonerisms, with celebrites such as Justin Bieber and Nick Jonas reportedly calling each other 'Bustin Jieber' and 'Jick Nonas'. After all, no-one ever said spoonerisms have to make sense …

Celebrity spoonerisms

Mike Baker (bike maker)
Shirley Bassey (burly chassis)
Justin Bieber (bustin jieber)
Kelly Brook (belly crook)
Gordon Brown (broaden gown)
Nick Jonas (jick nonas)
Gene Kelly (keen jelly)
Jude Law (lewd jaw)
Sarah Palin (para sailing)
Shiloh Pitt (pile o' s***)
Wesley Snipes (snesley wipes)
Paul Walker (wall porker)

German law prohibits invented and androgynous names but the UK has some of the most liberal rules on naming a baby in the world, with only names which are deemed to be offensive making it onto the banned list.

4

Registering a baby name

There are slightly different guidelines for registering births and names depending on where you live in the UK.

- **In England, Wales and Northern Ireland** a birth must be recorded within 42 days of delivery and if not done at the hospital it requires a visit to a register office.

- The birth certificate will be written in English if a child is born in England or Northern Ireland, and can be in both English and Welsh if they are born in Wales.

- If the birth is recorded at the hospital or registered in the same district, then birth certificates are usually issued straightaway, but if you end up going to a different office the certificate may be sent to you after a few days. This is important when applying for Child Benefits or registering your baby with a doctor as you will need a copy of the short birth certificate to apply.

- If the parents of a newborn are married, either parent can register a birth. However, if the parents are not married there are several ways to ensure both names are put on the birth certificate, including both parents being physically present at the registration or one parent submitting a declaration form in lieu of their presence. If neither parent can be present then someone who was present at the birth or someone who is now responsible for the child can also carry out the duty.

- After the registration, parents or those with parental responsibility also have the option of requesting a naming ceremony. These non-religious ceremonies are conducted by local authorities and can be a nice replacement for a baptism or Christening as adults outside of the family can be nominated to act in secular roles similar to godparents. A birth certificate is also needed for this event to take place.

- **In Scotland** births need to be registered within 21 days and can take place in any district. As well as either married parents being allowed to register the birth, relatives of those parents may also do the duty. The exception here is if the parents are not married. In this case the father may only register the birth if the mother is also present, a declaration form is submitted or a court agrees that he has parental responsibility just like any other adult. Parents of newborns in Scotland should take a card given to them at the hospital and a copy of their marriage certificate to the birth registration.

Useful websites:

Registering a birth in England and Wales: www.direct.gov.uk

Registering a birth in Northern Ireland: www.groni.gov.uk

Registering a birth in Scotland: www.gro-scotland.gov.uk

If you decide at a later stage you want to change details on the birth certificate there are procedures in place to help, although it is often a time-consuming process.

- It is worth remembering that if the father's details were not recorded on the original certificate or if the natural parents have married since the registration, a new birth certificate will have to be generated. Both changes require filling out an application form, available on the websites listed above.

- If you are unhappy with the forename you've chosen or it has been spelt incorrectly, you can change the birth record providing you have other documentation to prove this is the case. A passport or baptismal certificate is sufficient as they will show the correct spelling or commonly used forename and should be presented to the register office where the initial application was made.

- If you wish to change the surname of your baby it is only possible in two cases: either the spelling is incorrect or the details of the parents are being changed (such as the inclusion of the father or the parents now being married). Again, evidence and form submissions are needed to make any changes and a fee is usually incurred if a new certificate is required.

Keep in mind how difficult it may be for you to change your child's birth certificate at a later stage if you are in any way unsure about the choice you're about to make. However, also remember that if something unexpected happens and you need to make the change, it is possible. There are stories of drunken fathers registering the birth of their child alone with a name not agreed upon by the mother, much to her horror. As Robert Eisenschmidt said, 'I have a friend, Bill Land, who named his daughter Alison Wanda Land. His wife changed the name on the birth certificate when she found out.' So it is possible, though obviously not preferred.

> **Names are not always what they seem. The common Welsh name BZJXXLLWCP is pronounced Jackson.**
>
> Mark Twain

5

Naming twins, triplets and more

If you have discovered you are expecting multiples, congratulations! Naming multiples needn't be any different to naming a single child … unless you want it to be. You could stick to the same process everyone else does, by picking an individual name for each individual child. In January 2009, 'Octomom' Nadya Suleman chose eight different names for her octuplets, although they do all sound reasonably similar: Isaiah, Jeremiah, Jonah, Josiah, Maliah, McCai, Nariah, and Noah.

Another option is to go with a theme. Try anagrams or names in reverse, or give each child the same initials. You could even do this if you're not expecting multiples, like the Duggar family of Arkansas, USA, who have given each of their 19 children the initial 'J' – Joshua, Jana, John-David, Jill, Jessa, Jinger, Joseph, Josiah, Joy-Anna, Jedidiah, Jeremiah, Jason, James, Justin, Jackson, Johannah, Jennifer, Jordyn-Grace and Josie!

Mariah Carey and Nick Cannon chose to use names starting with the same letter when naming their twins. Before announcing the names, Nick posted a clue to the names on Twitter, 'So we r bout 2 reveal the actual names and b4 we tell em 2 our friends etc. both begin w/M's!!!!' The couple then announced the arrival of Monroe and Moroccan Scott.

A palindrome name is a name that is spelt the same backwards and forwards, as with Bob, Elle, Eve, and Hannah.

Twin names with the same meaning

Bernard and Brian (strong)
Daphne and Laura (laurel)
Deborah and Melissa (bee)
Dorcas and Tabitha (gazelle)
Elijah and Joel (God)
Eve and Zoe (life)
Irene and Salome (peace)
Lucius and Uri (light)
Lucy and Helen (light)
Sarah and Almira (princess)

Popular twin names in 2012

Daniel and David

Ella and Emma

Gabriella and Isabella

Isaac and Isaiah

Jacob and Joshua

Madison and Morgan

Taylor and Tyler

Of course, when's all said and done you can just stick to giving each child a name unique to them. For triplets, quads and more this is probably an easier choice than twisting your head around three names with the same meaning, or trying to create four anagrams you like for all of your babies. Some parents do like to use a theme though, such as going down the alphabet (think Alastair, Benjamin, Christopher, and David).

Names for triplets

Aidan, Diana and Nadia (anagrams)

Amber, Jade and Ruby (jewels)

Amy, May and Mya (anagrams)

Ava, Eva and Iva (similar)

Daisy, Lily and Rose (flowers)

Jay, Raven and Robin (birds)

Olive, Violet and Sage (colours)

Celebrity twin names of the past few years

Monroe and Moroccan Scott (Mariah Carey and Nick Cannon)

Darby and Sullivan (Patrick Dempsey and Jillian Fink)

Eddy and Nelson (Celine Dion and Rene Angelil)

Eden and Savannah (Marcia Cross and Tom Mahoney)

D'Lila Star and Jessie James (P Diddy and Kim Porter)

Hazel and Phinnaeus (Julia Roberts and Danny Moder)

Marion Loretta and Tabitha Hodge (Sarah Jessica Parker and Matthew Roderick)

Max and Bob (Charlie Sheen and Brooke Mueller)

Max and Emme (Jennifer Lopez and Marc Anthony)

Vivienne Marcheline and Knox Leon (Angelina Jolie and Brad Pitt)

"Names, once they are in common use, quickly become mere sounds, their etymology being buried, like so many of the earth's marvel beneath the dust of habit.

Salman Rushdie

part two

Boys' Names

A Boys' names

Aaron

Hebrew, meaning 'mountain of strength'.

Abasi

Egyptian, meaning 'male'.

Abdiel

Biblical, meaning 'servant of God'.

Abdul

Arabic, meaning 'servant'. Often followed with a suffix indicating who Abdul is the servant of (eg Abdul-Basit, 'servant of the creator').

Abdullah

Arabic, meaning 'servant of God'.

Abe

Hebrew, from Abraham, meaning 'father'.

Abel

Hebrew, meaning 'breath' or 'breathing spirit'. Associated with the biblical son of Adam and Eve who was killed by his brother Cain.

Abelard

German, meaning 'resolute'.

Aberforth

Gaelic, meaning 'mouth of the river Forth'. Name of Dumbledore's brother in the Harry Potter books.

A

Abheek

Indian, meaning 'fearless'.

Abhishek

Indian, meaning 'bath for a deity' or 'anointing'.

Abner

Hebrew, meaning 'father of light'.

Absalom

(alt. Absalon)

Hebrew, meaning 'father/leader of peace'.

Acacio

Greek, meaning 'thorny tree'. Now widely used in Spain.

Ace

English, meaning 'number one' or 'the best'.

Achilles

Greek, mythological hero of the Trojan war, whose heel was his only weak spot.

Achim

Hebrew, meaning 'God will establish' or Polish, meaning 'the Lord exalts'.

Ackerley

Old English, meaning 'oak meadow'. Often used as a surname.

Adalberto

Germanic/Spanish, meaning 'nobly bright'.

Adam

Hebrew, meaning 'man' or 'earth'. First man to walk the earth, accompanied by Eve.

Adão

Variant of Adam, meaning 'earth'.

Addison

Old English, meaning 'son of Adam'. Also used as a female name in the USA.

Ade

African, meaning 'peak' or 'pinnacle'.

A

Adelard

Teutonic, meaning 'brave' or 'noble'.

Adelbert

Old German form of Albert.

Aden

Gaelic, meaning 'fire'.

Adetokunbo

Yoruba, meaning 'the crown came from over the sea'.

Adin

Hebrew, meaning 'slender' or 'voluptuous'. Also Swahili, meaning 'ornamental'.

Aditya

Sanskrit, meaning 'belonging to the sun'.

Adlai

Hebrew, meaning 'God is just', or sometimes 'ornamental'.

Adler

Old German, meaning 'eagle'.

Adley

English, meaning 'son of Adam'.

Admon

Hebrew, variant of Adam meaning 'earth'. Also the name of a red peony.

Adolph
(alt. Adolf)

Old German, meaning 'noble majestic wolf'. Popularity of the name plummeted after the Second World War, for obvious reasons.

Adonis

Phoenician, meaning 'Lord'.

Movie inspirations

Austin *(Austin Powers)*
Don *(Singin' in the Rain)*
Edward (Twilight series)
Harry (Harry Potter series)
Jacob (Twilight series)
Jake *(Avatar)*
Korben *(The Fifth Element)*
Marty *(Back to the Future)*
Michael *(The Godfather)*
Renton *(Trainspotting)*
Wayne *(Wayne's World)*

A

Adrian

Latin, meaning 'from Hadria', a town in northern Italy.

Adriel

Hebrew, meaning 'of God's flock'.

Adyn

(alt. Adann, Ade, Aden)

Irish, meaning 'manly'.

Aeneas

Greek/Latin, meaning 'to praise'. Name of the hero who founded Rome in Virgil's *Aeneid*.

Aeson

Greek, father of Jason in Greek mythology.

Afonso

Portuguese, meaning 'eager noble warrior'.

Agamemnon

Greek, meaning 'leader of the assembly'. Figure in mythology, commanded the Greeks at the siege of Troy.

Agathon

Greek, meaning 'good' or 'superior'.

Agustin

Latin/Spanish, meaning 'venerated'.

Ahab

Hebrew, meaning 'father's brother'. Name of the obsessed captain in *Moby Dick*.

Ahijah

Hebrew, meaning 'brother of God' or 'friend of God'.

Ahmed

Arabic/Turkish, meaning 'worthy of praise'.

Aidan

(alt. Aiden)

Gaelic, meaning 'little fire'.

Aidric

Old English, meaning 'oaken'.

Airyck

Old Norse, from Eric, meaning 'eternal ruler'.

Ajani

African, meaning 'he fights for what he is'. Also Sanskrit, meaning 'of noble birth'.

Ajax

Greek, meaning 'mourner of the Earth'. Another Greek hero from the siege of Troy.

Ajay

Indian, meaning 'unconquerable'.

Ajit

Indian, meaning 'invincible'.

Akeem

Arabic, meaning 'wise or insightful'.

Akio

Japanese, meaning 'bright man'.

Akira

Japanese, meaning 'intelligent'.

Akiva

Hebrew, meaning 'to protect' or 'to shelter'.

Akon

American, made popular by the famous rapper charting in 2008/2009.

Aksel

Hebrew/Danish, meaning 'father of peace'.

Aladdin

Arabic, meaning 'servant of Allah'. From the medieval story in *Arabian Nights*.

Alan

(alt. Allan, Allen, Allyn, Alun)

Gaelic, meaning 'rock'.

Alaric

Old German, meaning 'noble regal ruler'.

Alastair

(alt. Alasdair, Allister)

Greek/Gaelic, meaning 'defending men'.

Alban

Latin, meaning 'from Alba'. Also the name of Saint Alban, the first British Christian martyr.

A

Alberic

Germanic, meaning 'Elfin king'.

Albert

Old German, meaning 'noble, bright, famous'.

Albin

Latin, meaning 'white'.

Albus

Latin, variant of Albin meaning 'white'. Also the Christian name of Albus Dumbledore, headmaster of Hogwarts School in the Harry Potter series.

Alcaeus

Greek, meaning 'strength'.

Alden

Old English, meaning 'old friend'.

Aldis

English, meaning 'from the old house'.

Aldo

Italian, meaning 'old' or 'elder'.

Aldric

English, meaning 'old King'.

Alec

(alt. Alek)

English, meaning 'defending men'.

Aled

Welsh, meaning 'child' or 'offspring'.

Aleron

(alt. Aileron, Alerun, Ailerun)

Latin, meaning 'child with wings'.

Alessio

Italian, meaning 'defender'.

Alexander

(alt. Alexandro, Alessandro)

Greek, meaning 'defending men'.

Alexei

Russian, meaning 'defender'.

Alfonso

Germanic/Spanish, meaning 'noble and prompt, ready to struggle'.

A

Alford

Old English, meaning 'old river/ford'.

Alfred

(alt. Alf, Alfi)

English, meaning 'elf' or 'magical counsel'.

Algernon

French, meaning 'with a moustache'.

Ali

(alt. Allie)

Arabic, meaning 'noble, sublime'.

Alois

German, meaning 'famous warrior'.

Alok

Indian, meaning 'cry of triumph'.

Alon

Jewish, meaning 'oak tree'.

Alonso

(alt. Alonzo)

Germanic, meaning 'noble and ready'.

Aloysius

Italian saint's name, meaning 'fame and war'.

Alpha

First letter of the Greek alphabet.

Alphaeus

Hebrew, meaning 'changing'.

Alpin

Gaelic, meaning 'related to the Alps'.

Altair

Arabic, meaning 'flying' or 'bird'.

Alter

Yiddish, meaning 'old man'.

Alton

Old English, meaning 'old town'.

Alva

Latin, meaning 'white'.

A

Alvie

German, meaning 'army of elves'.

Alvin

English, meaning 'friend of elves'.

Alwyn

Welsh, meaning 'wise friend'. May also come from the River Alwen in Wales.

Amachi

African, meaning 'who knows what God has brought us through this child'.

Amadeus

Latin, meaning 'God's love'.

Amadi

African, meaning 'appeared destined to die at birth'.

Amado

Spanish, meaning 'God's love'.

Amador

Spanish, meaning 'one who loves'.

Amari

Hebrew, meaning 'given by God'.

Amarion

Arabic, meaning 'populous, flushing'.

Amasa

Hebrew, meaning 'burden'.

Ambrose

Greek, meaning 'undying, immortal'.

Americo

Germanic, meaning 'ever powerful in battle'.

Amias

Latin, meaning 'loved'.

Amil

African, meaning 'effective'.

Amir

Hebrew, meaning 'prince' or 'treetop'.

Amit

Hindu, meaning 'friend'.

A

Ammon
Egyptian, meaning 'the hidden one'.

Amory
German/English, meaning 'work' and 'power'.

Amos
Hebrew, meaning 'encumbered' or 'burdened'.

Anacletus
Latin, meaning 'called back' or 'invoked'.

Anakin
American, meaning 'warrior'. Made famous by Anakin Skywalker in the Star Wars films.

Ananias
Greek/Italian, meaning 'answered by the Lord'.

Anastasius
Latin, meaning 'resurrection'.

Anat
Jewish, meaning 'water spring'.

Anatole
Greek, meaning 'cynical but without malice'.

Anders
Greek, meaning 'lion man'.

Anderson
English, meaning 'male'.

Andrew
(alt. Andreas)
Greek, meaning 'man' or 'warrior'.

Androcles
Greek, meaning 'glory of a warrior'.

Angel
Greek, meaning 'messenger'.

Angus
Scottish, meaning 'one choice'.

Anil
Sanskrit, meaning 'air' or 'wind'.

Anselm
German, meaning 'helmet of God'.

A

Anson
English, meaning 'son of Agnes'.

Anthony
English, from the old Roman family name.

Antipas
Israeli, meaning 'for all or against all'.

Antwan
Old English, meaning 'flower'.

Apollo
Greek, meaning 'to destroy'. Greek god of the sun.

Apostolos
Greek, meaning 'apostle'.

Ara
Armenian. Ara was a legendary king.

Aragorn
Literary, used by Tolkien in *The Lord of the Rings* trilogy.

Aram
Hebrew, meaning 'Royal Highness'.

Aramis
Latin, meaning 'swordsman'.

Arcadio
Greek/Spanish, from a place in ancient Greece. The word 'Arcadia' (meaning paradise) comes from this.

Archibald
(alt. Archie)
Old German, meaning 'genuine, bold, brave'.

Ardell
Latin, meaning 'eager, burning with enthusiasm'.

Arden
Celtic, meaning 'high'.

Ares
Greek, meaning 'ruin'. Son of Zeus and Greek god of war.

A

Ari

Hebrew, meaning 'lion' or 'eagle'.

Arias

Germanic, meaning 'lion'.

Aric

English, meaning 'merciful ruler'.

Ariel

Hebrew, meaning 'lion of God'. One of the archangels, the angel of healing and new beginnings.

Arild

Old Norse, meaning 'battle commander'.

Aris

Greek, meaning 'best figure'.

Ariston

Greek, meaning 'the best'.

Aristotle

Greek, meaning 'best'. Also a famous philosopher.

Arjun

Sanskrit, meaning 'white'.

Arkady

Greek, region of central Greece.

Arlan

Gaelic, meaning 'pledge' or 'oath'.

Arlie

Old English place name, meaning 'eagle wood'.

Arlis

Hebrew, meaning 'pledge'.

Arlo

Spanish, meaning 'barberry tree'.

Armand

Old German, meaning 'soldier'.

Armani

Same origin as Armand meaning 'soldier'. Nowadays closely associated with the Italian designer.

A

Arnaldo
Spanish, meaning 'eagle power'.

Arnav
Indian, meaning 'the sea'.

Arnold
Old German, meaning 'eagle ruler'.

Arrow
English, from the common word denoting weaponry.

Art
Irish, name of a warrior in Irish mythology, Art Oenfer (Art the Lonely).

Arthur
(alt. Artie, Artis)

Celtic, probably from 'artos', meaning 'bear'. Made famous by the tales of King Arthur and the Knights of the Round Table.

Arvel
From the Welsh 'Arwel', meaning 'wept over'.

Arvid
English, meaning 'eagle in the woods'.

Arvind
Indian, meaning 'red lotus'.

Arvo
Finnish, meaning 'value' or 'worth'.

Arwen
Welsh, meaning 'fair' or 'fine'.

Asa
Hebrew, meaning 'doctor' or 'healer'.

Asante
African, meaning 'thank you'.

Asher
Hebrew, meaning 'fortunate' or 'lucky'.

Ashley
Old English, meaning 'ash meadow'.

Ashok
Sanskrit, meaning 'not causing sorrow'.

Ashton

English, meaning 'settlement in the ash-tree grove'.

Aslan

Turkish, meaning 'lion'. Strongly associated with the lion from C. S. Lewis' *The Lion, the Witch, and the Wardrobe.*

Asriel

Hebrew, meaning 'help of God'.

Astrophel

Latin, meaning 'star lover'.

Athanasios

Greek, meaning 'eternal life'.

Atílio

Portuguese, meaning 'father'.

Atlas

Greek, meaning 'to carry'. In Greek mythology Atlas was a Titan forced to carry the weight of the heavens.

Atlee

Hebrew, meaning 'God is just'.

Atticus

Latin, meaning 'from Athens'.

Auberon

Old German, meaning 'royal bear'.

Aubrey

Old German, meaning 'power'.

Auden

Old English, meaning 'old friend'.

Audie

Old English, meaning 'noble strength'.

Augustas

(alt. Augustus)

Latin, meaning 'venerated'.

Aurelien

French, meaning 'golden'.

Austin

Latin, meaning 'venerated'. Also a city in the state of Texas in the USA.

A

Avi

Hebrew, meaning 'father of a multitude of nations'.

Avery

(alt. Avrie, Averey, Averie)

English, meaning 'wise ruler'.

Awnan

Irish, meaning 'little Adam'.

Axel

Hebrew, meaning 'father is peace'. Made famous by Guns 'n' Roses front man Axl Rose.

Ayers

(alt. Ayer, Aires, Aire)

English, meaning 'heir to a fortune'.

Azarel

Hebrew, meaning 'helped by God'.

Azaryah

Hebrew, meaning 'helped by God'.

Azriel

Hebrew, meaning 'God is my help'.

Azuko

African, meaning 'past glory'.

 Boys' names

Baden

German, meaning 'battle'.

Bailey

English, meaning 'bailiff'.

Baird

Scottish, meaning 'poet' or 'one who sings ballads'.

Bakari

Swahili, meaning 'hope' or 'promise'.

Baker

English, from the word 'baker'.

Baldwin

Old French, meaning 'bold, brave friend'.

Balin

Old English. Balin was one of the Knights of the Round Table.

Balthazar

Babylonian, meaning 'protect the King'.

Balvinder

Hindu, meaning 'merciful, compassionate'.

Bannon

Irish, meaning descendant of O'Banain. Also a river in Wales.

Barack

African, meaning 'blessed'. Made popular by US President Barack Obama.

B

Barclay

Old English, meaning 'birch tree meadow'. Also Persian, meaning 'messenger'.

Barker

Old English, meaning 'shepherd'.

Barnaby

(alt. Barney)

Greek, meaning 'son of consolation'.

Barnard

English, meaning 'strong as a bear'.

Baron

Old English, meaning 'young warrior'.

Barrett

English, meaning 'strong as a bear'.

Barron

Old German, meaning 'old clearing'.

Barry

Irish Gaelic, meaning 'fair haired'. Also a town in South Wales, made popular by the BBC television series Gavin and Stacey.

Bart

Hebrew, from Bartholomew, meaning 'son of the farmer'. Made popular by the famous American TV character Bart Simpson.

Barton

Old English, meaning 'barley settlement'.

Baruch

Hebrew, meaning 'blessed'.

Barzillai

Hebrew, meaning 'my iron'.

Bashir

Arabic, meaning 'well-educated' and 'wise'.

Basil

Greek, meaning 'royal, kingly'.

B

Basim
Arabic, meaning 'smile'.

Bastien
Greek, meaning 'revered'.

Baxter
Old English, meaning 'baker'.

Bayard
French, meaning 'auburn haired'.

Bayre
American, meaning 'beautiful'.

Bayo
Nigerian, meaning 'to find joy'.

Baz
Irish Gaelic, meaning 'fair-haired'.

Beau
French, meaning 'handsome'.

Beck
Old Norse, meaning 'stream'.

Beckett
Old English, meaning 'beehive' or 'bee cottage'. Associated with the Irish writer Samuel Beckett.

Beckham
English, meaning 'homestead by the stream'. Made famous by David and Victoria Beckham.

Béla
Hungarian, meaning 'within'.

Belarius
Shakespearean, meaning 'a banished lord'.

Benedict
Latin, meaning 'blessed'.

Biblical names

Abel
Cain
Eli
Joseph
Luke
Mark
Moses
Paul
Peter
Solomon

B

Benicio
Spanish, meaning 'benevolent'.

Benjamin
(alt. Ben)
Hebrew, meaning 'son of the south'.

Bennett
French/Latin vernacular form of Benedict, meaning 'blessed'.

Benoit
French form of Benedict, meaning 'blessed'.

Benson
English, meaning 'son of Ben'. Also linked to the village of Benson in Oxfordshire.

Bentley
Old English, meaning 'bent grass meadow'.

Benton
Old English, meaning 'town in the bent grass'.

Beriah
Hebrew, meaning 'in fellowship' or 'in envy'.

Bernard
(alt. Bernie)
Germanic, meaning 'strong, brave bear'.

Berry
Old English, meaning 'berry'.

Bert
(alt. Bertram/Bertrand)
Old English, meaning 'illustrious'.

Berton
Old English, meaning 'bright settlement'.

Bevan
Welsh, meaning 'son of Evan'.

Bilal
Arabic, meaning 'wetting, refreshing'.

Bill
(alt. Billy)
English, from William, meaning 'determined' or 'resolute'.

Birch
Old English, meaning 'bright' or 'shining'.

B

Birger
Norwegian, meaning 'rescue'.

Bishop
Old English, meaning 'bishop'.

Bjorn
Old Norse, meaning 'bear'.

Bladen
Hebrew, meaning 'hero'.

Blaine
Irish Gaelic, meaning 'yellow'.

Blair
English, meaning 'plain'.

Blaise
French, meaning 'lisp' or 'stutter'.

Blake
Old English, meaning 'dark, black'.

Blas
(alt. Blaze)
German, meaning 'firebrand'.

Bo
Scandinavian, short form of Robert, meaning 'bright fame'.

Boaz
Hebrew, meaning 'swiftness' or 'strength'.

Bob
(alt. Bobby)
Old German, from Robert meaning 'bright fame'.

Boden
(alt. Bodie)
Scandinavian, meaning 'shelter'.

Bogumil
Slavic, meaning 'God favour'.

Bolivar
Spanish, meaning 'the bank of the river'.

Bond
Old English, meaning 'peasant farmer'.

Boris
Slavic, meaning 'battle glory'.

B

Saints' names

Aidan
Bernard
Francis
Gabriel
Kieran
Nicholas
Patrick
Stephen
Thomas
Vincent

Bosten
English, meaning 'town by the woods'.

Botolf
English, meaning 'wolf'.

Bowen
Welsh, meaning 'son of Owen'.

Boyd
Scottish Gaelic, meaning 'yellow'.

Brad
(alt. Bradley)
Old English, meaning 'broad' or 'wide'.

Brady
Irish, meaning 'large-chested'.

Bradyn
Gaelic, meaning 'descendant of Bradan'.

Bram
Gaelic, meaning 'raven'.

Brandon
Old English, meaning 'gorse'.

Brandt
Old English, meaning 'beacon'.

Brannon
Gaelic, meaning 'raven'.

Branson
English, meaning 'son of Brand'.

Brant
Old English, meaning 'hill'.

Braulio
Greek, meaning 'shining'.

Brendan
Gaelic, meaning 'prince'.

Brennan
Gaelic, meaning 'teardrop'.

Brenton
English, from Brent, meaning 'hill'.

Brett
English, meaning 'a brewer'.

Brewster
(alt. Brew, Brewer)
English, meaning 'a brewer'.

Brian
Gaelic, meaning 'high' or 'noble'.

Brice
Latin, meaning 'speckled'.

Brier
French, meaning 'heather'.

Brock
Old English, meaning 'badger'.

Broderick
English, meaning 'ruler'.

Brody
Gaelic, meaning both 'ditch' and 'brother'.

Brogan
Irish, meaning 'sturdy shoe'.

Bronwyn
Welsh, meaning 'white breasted'.

Brook
English, meaning 'stream'.

Bruce
Scottish, meaning 'high' or 'noble'.

Bruno
Germanic, meaning 'brown'.

Brewster
(alt. Brutus)
Latin, meaning 'dim-wit'. The name of Julius Caesar's assassin.

Bryant
English variant of Brian, meaning 'high' or 'noble'.

B

Bryce
Scottish, meaning 'of Britain'.

Brycen
Scottish, meaning 'son of Bryce'.

Bryden
Irish, meaning 'strong one'.

Bryson
Welsh, meaning 'descendant of Brice'.

Bubba
American, meaning 'boy'.

Buck
American, meaning 'goat' or 'deer'.

Bud
(alt. Buddy)
American, meaning 'friend'.

Burdett
Middle English, meaning 'bird'.

Burgess
(alt. Burges, Burgiss, Berje)
English, meaning 'business'.

Burke
French, meaning 'fortified settlement'.

Burl
French, meaning 'knotty wood'.

Buzz
American, shortened form of Busby, meaning 'village in the thicket'. Associated with the astronaut Buzz Aldrin.

Byron
Old English, meaning 'barn'. Made famous by the poet Lord Byron.

Sci-fi names
Anakin
Balin
Chike
Dante
Faizah
Fola
Hahzara
Kanene
Kibo
Shatea
Umi

C Boys' names

Cabot
Old English, meaning 'to sail'.

Cadby
(alt. Cadbey, Cadbee, Cadbie)
English, meaning 'soldier's colony'.

Cade
(alt. Caden)
English, meaning 'round, lumpy'.

Cadence
Latin, meaning 'with rhythm'.

Cadogan
Welsh, meaning 'battle glory and honour'.

Caedmon
Celtic, meaning 'wise warrior'.

Caelan
Gaelic, from St Columba.

Caerwyn
(alt. Carwyn, Gerwyn)
Welsh, meaning 'white fort' or 'settlement'.

Caesar
Latin, meaning 'head of hair'. Made famous by the first Roman emperor Julius Caesar.

Caetano
Portuguese, meaning 'from Gaeta, Italy.

Cagney
Irish, meaning 'successor of the advocate'.

C

Caiden
Arabic, meaning 'companion'.

Caillou
French, meaning 'pebble'.

Cain
Hebrew, brother of Abel.

Cainan
Hebrew, meaning 'possessor' or 'purchaser'.

Cairo
Egyptian city.

Cal
Short form of names beginning Cal-.

Calder
Scottish, meaning 'rough waters'.

Caleb
Hebrew, meaning 'dog'.

Calen
From Caleb, meaning 'dog'.

Calhoun
Irish, meaning 'slight woods'.

Calix
Greek, meaning 'very handsome'.

Callahan
Irish, meaning 'contention' or 'strife'.

Callum
Gaelic, meaning 'dove'.

Calvin
French, meaning 'little bald one'.

Camden
Gaelic, meaning 'winding valley'. Also an area of north London.

Cameron
Scottish Gaelic, meaning 'crooked nose'.

Camillo
Latin, meaning 'free born' or 'noble'.

Campbell
Scottish Gaelic, meaning 'crooked mouth'.

C

Canaan

Hebrew, meaning 'to be humbled'.

Candido

Latin, meaning 'candid' or 'honest'.

Cannon

French, meaning 'of the church'.

Canton

French, 'dweller of corner'. Also name given to areas of Switzerland.

Canute

(alt. Cnut, Cnute)
Scandinavian, meaning 'knot'. Name of the King of England in the 11th century.

Cappy

Italian, meaning 'lucky'.

Carden

Old English, meaning 'wool carder'.

Carey

Gaelic, meaning 'love'.

Carl

Old Norse, meaning 'free man'.

Carlo

Italian form of Carl, meaning 'free man'.

Carlos

Spanish form of Carl, meaning 'free man'.

Carlton

Old English, meaning 'free peasant settlement'.

Carmelo

Latin, meaning 'garden' or 'orchard'.

Carmen

Latin/Spanish, meaning 'song'.

Carmine

Latin, meaning 'song'.

Carnell

English, meaning 'defender of the castle'.

Carson

(alt. Carsten)
Scottish, meaning 'marsh-dwellers'.

Carter

Old English, meaning 'transporter of goods'.

C

Cary
Old Celtic river name. Also means 'love'.

Case
(alt. Casey)
Irish Gaelic, meaning 'alert' or 'watchful'.

Cash
Latin, shortened form of Cassius, meaning 'vain'.

Casimer
Slavic, meaning 'famous destroyer of peace'.

Cason
Latin, from Cassius, meaning 'empty' or 'hollow'.

Casper
Persian, meaning 'treasurer'.

Caspian
English, meaning 'of the Caspy people'. From the Caspian Sea.

Cassidy
Gaelic, meaning 'curly haired'.

Cassius
(alt. Cassio)
Latin, meaning 'empty, hollow'.

Cathal
Celtic, meaning 'battle rule'.

Cato
Latin, meaning 'all-knowing'.

TV personality names

Anthony (McPartlin)
Bruce (Forsyth)
Chris (Evans, Moyles)
Declan (Donnelly)
Dermot (O'Leary)
Graham (Norton)
Louis (Walsh)
Michael (McIntyre)
Phillip (Schofield)
Piers (Morgan)
Simon (Cowell)
Vernon (Kay)

C

Cecil

Latin, meaning 'blind'.

Cedar

English, from the name of an evergreen tree.

Cedric

Welsh, meaning 'spectacular bounty'.

Celestino

Spanish/Italian, meaning 'heavenly'.

Celesto
(alt. Celindo)

Latin, meaning 'heaven sent'.

Chad
(alt. Chadrick)

Old English, meaning 'warlike, warrior'.

Chaim

Hebrew, meaning 'life'.

Champion

English, from the word 'champion', meaning 'warrior'.

Chance

English, from the word 'chance' meaning 'good fortune'.

Chandler

Old English, meaning 'candle maker and seller'.

Charles
(alt. Charlie)

Old German, meaning 'free man'.

Chaska

Native American name usually given to first son.

Che

Spanish, shortened form of José. Made famous by Che Guevara.

Chesley

Old English, meaning 'camp on the meadow'.

Chester

Latin, meaning 'camp of soldiers'.

Chilton
(alt. Chillron, Chilly, Chilt)

English, meaning 'tranquil'.

C

Chima
Old English, meaning 'hilly land'.

Christian
English, from the word 'Christian'.

Christophe
French variant of Christopher, meaning 'bearing Christ inside'.

Christopher
Greek, meaning 'bearing Christ inside'.

Cian
Irish, meaning 'ancient'.

Ciaran
Irish, meaning 'black'.

Cicero
Latin, meaning 'chickpea'. Famous Roman philosopher and orator.

Cimarron
City in western Kansas.

Ciprian
Latin, meaning 'from Cyprus'.

Ciro
Spanish, meaning 'sun'.

Clancy
Old Irish, meaning 'red warrior'.

Clarence
Latin, meaning 'one who lives near the river Clare'.

Clark
Latin, meaning 'clerk'.

Claude
(alt. Claudie, Claudio, Claudius)
Latin, meaning 'lame'.

Claus
Variant of Nicholas, meaning 'people of victory'.

Clay
English, from the word 'clay'.

Clement
(alt. Clem)
Latin, meaning 'merciful'.

Cleo
Greek, meaning 'glory'.

C

Cletus

Greek, meaning 'illustrious'.

Cliff

(alt. Clifford, Clifton)

English, from the word 'cliff'.

Clint

(alt. Clinton)

Old English, meaning 'fenced settlement'.

Clive

Old English, meaning 'cliff' or 'slope'.

Clyde

Scottish, from the river in Glasgow.

Coby

(alt. Cody, Colby)

Irish, meaning 'son of Oda'.

Colden

Old English, meaning 'dark valley'.

Cole

Old French, meaning 'coal black'.

Coley

Old English, meaning 'coal black'.

Colin

Gaelic, meaning 'young creature'.

Colson

Old English, meaning 'coal black'.

Colton

English, meaning 'swarthy'.

Columbus

Latin, meaning 'dove'.

Colwyn

Welsh, from the river in Wales.

Conan

Gaelic, meaning 'wolf'.

Conley

Gaelic, meaning 'sensible'.

Connell

(alt. Connolly)

Irish, meaning 'high' or 'mighty'.

C

Connor
(alt. Conrad, Conroy)
Irish, meaning 'lover of hounds'.

Constant
(alt. Constantine)
English, from the word 'constant'.

Cooper
Old English, meaning 'barrel maker'.

Corban
Hebrew, meaning 'dedicated and belonging to God'.

Corbett
(alt. Corbin, Corby)
Norman French, meaning 'young crow'.

Cordell
Old English, meaning 'cord maker'.

Corey
(alt. Cory)
Gaelic, meaning 'hill hollow'.

Corin
Latin, meaning 'spear'.

Corliss
(alt. Corlis, Corlyss, Corlys)
English, meaning 'benevolent'.

Cormac
Gaelic, meaning 'impure son'.

Cornelius
(alt. Cornell)
Latin, meaning 'horn'.

Cortez
Spanish, meaning 'courteous'.

Uncommon three-syllable names

Alastair
Barnaby
Dominic
Dorian
Elijah
Elliot
Lancelot
Roberto
Theodore

Corwin

Old English, meaning 'heart's friend' or 'companion'.

Cosimo

(alt. Cosme, Cosmo)

Italian, meaning 'order' or 'beauty'.

Coty

French, meaning 'riverbank'.

Coulter

English, meaning 'young horse'.

Courtney

Old English, meaning 'domain of Curtis'.

Cowan

Gaelic, meaning 'hollow in the hill'.

Craig

Welsh, meaning 'rock'.

Crispin

Latin, meaning 'curly haired'.

Croix

French, meaning 'cross'.

Cruz

Spanish, meaning 'cross'. Made famous by David and Victoria Beckham's son.

Cullen

Gaelic, meaning 'handsome'.

Curran

Gaelic, meaning 'dagger' or 'hero'.

Curtis

(alt. Curt)

Old French, meaning 'courteous'.

Cutler

Old English, meaning 'knife maker'.

Cyprian

English, meaning 'from Cyprus'.

Cyril

Greek, meaning 'master' or 'Lord'.

Cyrus

Persian, meaning 'Lord'.

Prime Ministers' names

Anthony (Eden, Blair)

Arthur (Wellesley, Balfour, Chamberlain)

David (Cameron)

Charles (Wentworth, Grey)

George (Grenville, Canning, Gordon)

Gordon (Brown)

Harold (Macmillan, Wilson)

Henry (Pelham, Fitzroy, Addington, Temple,
   Campbell-Bannerman, Asquith)

James (Balfour, MacDonald, Wilson)

John (Stuart, Russell, Major)

Robert (Walpole, Jenkinson, Peel, Gascoyne-Cecil)

Spencer (Crompton, Perceval)

William (Cavendish, Pitt (Elder and Younger),
   Wyndham, Lamb, Gladstone)

 **Boys' names**

Dabeel
(alt. Dabee, Dabie, Daby)
Indian, meaning 'warrior'.

Dafydd
Welsh, meaning 'beloved'.
Made famous by the character
in the BBC television series
Little Britain.

Daichi
Japanese, meaning 'great
wisdom'.

Daire
(alt. Daer, Daere, Dair)
Irish, meaning 'wealthy'.

Daisuke
Japanese, meaning
'lionhearted'.

Dakari
African, meaning 'happy'.

Dale
Old English, meaning 'valley'.

Dallin
English, meaning 'dweller in the
valley'.

Dalton
English, meaning 'town in the
valley'.

Daly
Gaelic, meaning 'assembly'.

Damarion
Greek, meaning 'gentle'.

D

Damian
(alt. Damon)
Greek, meaning 'to tame, subdue'.

Dane
Old English, meaning 'from Denmark'.

Daniel
(alt. Dan, Danny)
Hebrew, meaning 'God is my judge'.

Dante
Latin, meaning 'lasting'. Associated with the Italian 13th century poet Dante Alighieri author of *The Divine Comdey*.

Darby
Irish, meaning 'without envy'.

Darcy
Gaelic, meaning 'dark'. Associated with Jane Austen's Mr Darcy, and the parody of this character in *Bridget Jones' Diary*.

Dario
(alt. Darius)
Greek, meaning 'kingly'.

Darnell
Old English, meaning 'the hidden spot'.

Darragh
Irish, meaning 'dark oak'.

Darrell
(alt. Daryl)
Old English, meaning 'open'.

Darren
(alt. Darrian)
Gaelic, meaning 'great'.

Darrick
Old German, meaning 'power of the tribe'.

Darshan
Hindi, meaning 'vision'.

Darwin
Old English, meaning 'dear friend'. Often associated with the naturalist Charles Darwin.

Dason
Native American, meaning 'chief'.

D

Dash
(alt. Dashawn)

American, meaning 'enlightened one'.

Dashiell
French, meaning 'page boy'.

David
(alt. Dave, Davey, Davie, Davian)

Hebrew, meaning 'beloved'.

Davis
Old English, meaning 'son of David'.

Dawson
Old English, meaning 'son of David'.

Dax
(alt. Daxton)

French, once a town in south-western France. Now associated with the *Star Trek* character.

Dayal
Indian, meaning 'kind'.

Dayton
Old English, meaning 'David's place'.

Dean
Old English, meaning 'valley'.

Declan
Irish, meaning 'full of goodness'.

Dedric
Old English, meaning 'gifted ruler'.

Deepak
(alt. Deepan)

Indian, meaning 'illumination'.

Del
(alt. Delano, Delbert, Dell)

Old English, meaning 'bright shining one'.

Delaney
Irish, meaning 'dark challenge'.

Demetrius
Greek, meaning 'harvest lover'.

Dempsey
Irish, meaning 'proud'.

Denham
(alt. Denholm)

Old English, meaning 'valley settlement'.

D

Old name, new fashion?

Bertrand
Dexter
Felix
Hector
Jefferson
Norris
Pierce
Reginald
Ulysses
Winston

Dennis
(alt. Denny, Denton)
English, meaning 'follower of Dionysius'.

Denzil
(alt. Denzel)
English, meaning 'fort'. Also a town in Cornwall.

Deon
Greek, meaning 'of Zeus'.

Derek
English, meaning 'power of the tribe'.

Dermot
Irish, meaning 'free man'.

Desmond
Irish, meaning 'from south Munster'.

Destin
French, meaning 'destiny'.

Devyn
Irish, meaning 'poet'.

Dewey
Welsh, from Dewi (David).

Dexter
(alt. Dex)
Latin, meaning 'right-handed'.

Diallo
(alt. Dialo)
African, meaning 'bold'.

Dick
(alt. Dickie, Dickon)
From Richard, meaning 'powerful leader'.

Didier
French, meaning 'much desired'.

Diego

Spanish, meaning 'supplanter'.

Dietrich

Old German, meaning 'power of the tribe'.

Diggory

English, meaning 'dyke'.

Dilbert

English, meaning 'day-bright'.

Dimitri

(alt. Dimitrios, Dimitris)

Greek, meaning 'Prince'.

Dino

Diminutive of Dean, meaning 'valley'.

Dion

Greek, short form of Dionysius, the Greek god of wine.

Dirk

Variant of Derek, meaning 'power of the tribe'.

Divakar

Sanskrit, meaning 'the sun'.

Dobbin

Diminutive of Robert, meaning 'bright fame'.

Dominic

Latin, meaning 'Lord'.

Donald

(alt. Don, Donal, Donaldo)

Gaelic, meaning 'great chief'.

Donato

Italian, meaning 'gift'.

Donnell

(alt. Donnie, Donny)

Gaelic, meaning 'world fighter'.

Donovan

Gaelic, meaning 'dark-haired chief'.

Doran

Gaelic, meaning 'exile'.

Dorian

Greek, meaning 'descendant of Doris'. Name of the title character in Oscar Wilde's *The Picutre of Dorian Gray*.

D

Douglas
(alt. Dougal, Dougie)
Scottish, meaning 'black river'.

Doyle
Irish, meaning 'foreigner'.

Draco
Latin, meaning 'dragon'. Made popular by the character Draco Malfoy in the Harry Potter series.

Drake
Greek, meaning 'dragon'.

Drew
Shortened form of Andrew, Greek, meaning 'man' or 'warrior'.

Dryden
English, meaning 'dry town'.

Dudley
Old English, meaning 'people's field'. Also a town in the West Midlands, and the name of Harry Potter's cousin.

Duff
Gaelic, meaning 'swarthy'.

Duke
Latin, meaning 'leader'.

Duncan
Scottish, meaning 'dark warrior'.

Dustin
(alt. Dusty)
French, meaning 'brave warrior'.

Dwayne
Irish Gaelic, meaning 'swarthy'.

Dwight
Flemish, meaning 'blond'.

Dwyer
Gaelic, meaning 'dark wise one'.

Dyani
Native American, meaning 'eagle'.

Dylan
(alt. Dillon)
Welsh, meaning 'son of the sea'.

E

Boys' names

Eagan
Irish, meaning 'fiery'.

Eamon
(alt. Eames)
Irish, meaning 'wealthy protector'.

Earl
(alt. Earle, Errol)
English, meaning 'nobleman, warrior, prince'.

Ebb
Shortened form of Ebenezer, meaning 'stone of help'.

Ebenezer
Hebrew, meaning 'stone of help'.

Ed
(alt. Edd, Eddie, Eddy)
Shortened form of Edward, meaning 'wealthy guard'.

Edgar
(alt. Elgar)
Old English, meaning 'wealthy spear'.

Edison
English, meaning 'son of Edward'.

Edmund
English, meaning 'wealthy protector'.

Edric
Old English, meaning 'rich and powerful'.

E

Edsel
Old German, meaning 'noble'.

Edward
(alt. Eduardo)
Old English, meaning 'wealthy guard'.

Edwin
English, meaning 'wealthy friend'.

Efrain
Hebrew, meaning 'fruitful'.

Egan
Irish, meaning 'fire'.

Eilif
(alt. Elif, Eilyg, Elyf)
Norse, meaning 'immortal'.

Einar
Old Norse, meaning 'battle leader'.

Eladio
Greek, meaning 'Greek'.

Elam
Hebrew, meaning 'eternal'.

Elbert
Old English, meaning 'famous'.

Eldon
Old English, meaning 'Ella's hill'.

Eldred
(alt. Eldridge)
Old English, meaning 'old venerable counsel'.

Elgin
Old English, meaning 'high minded'.

Eli
(alt. Eliah)
Hebrew, meaning 'high'.

Elias
(alt. Elijah)
Hebrew, meaning 'the Lord is my God'.

Elio
Spanish, meaning 'the Lord is my God'.

Ellery
Old English, meaning 'elder tree'.

Elliott
Spanish, variant of Elio, meaning 'the Lord is my God'.

Ellis
Welsh, variant of Elio, meaning 'the Lord is my God'.

E

Ellison
English, meaning 'son of Ellis'.

Elmer
(alt. Elmo)
Old English, meaning 'noble';
Arabic, meaning 'aristocratic'.

Elmo
(alt. Ellmo, Elmon)
Greek, meaning 'gregarious'. One
of the characters in the children's
television series *Sesame Street*.

Elon
Hebrew, meaning 'oak tree'.

Elroy
French, meaning 'king'.

Elton
Old English, meaning 'Ella's town'.

Elvin
English, meaning 'elf-like'.

Elvis
Figure in Norse mythology. Made
famous by the singer Elvis Presley.

Emanuel
Hebrew, meaning 'God is with us'.

Emeric
German, meaning 'work rule'.

Emile
(alt. Emiliano, Emilio)
Latin, meaning 'eager'.

Emlyn
Welsh, name of town,
Newcastle Emlyn, in West
Wales.

Emmett
English, meaning 'universal'.

Emrys
Welsh, meaning 'immortal'.

Eneco
Spanish, meaning 'fiery one'.

Enoch
Hebrew, meaning 'dedicated'.

Enrico
(alt. Enrique)
Italian, form of Henry, meaning
'home ruler'.

Enzo
Italian, short for Lorenzo,
meaning 'laurel'.

E

Eoghan
(alt. Eoin)
Irish form of Owen, meaning 'well born' or 'noble'.

Eoin
Irish, meaning 'God is gracious'.

Ephron
(alt. Effron)
Hebrew, meaning 'dust'.

Erasmo
(alt. Erasmus)
Greek, meaning 'to love'.

Eric
Old Norse, meaning 'ruler'.

Ernest
(alt. Ernesto, Ernie, Ernst)
Old German, meaning 'serious'.

Errol
English, meaning 'boar wolf'.

Erskine
Scottish, meaning 'high cliff'. Also a place in Scotland.

Erwin
Old English, meaning 'boar friend'.

Eryx
Greek, meaning 'boxer'.

Ethan
(alt. Etienne)
Hebrew, meaning 'long lived'.

Eugene
Greek, meaning 'well-born'.

Evan
Welsh, meaning 'God is good'.

Everard
Old English, meaning 'strong boar'.

Everett
English, meaning 'strong boar'.

Ewald
(alt. Ewan, Ewell)
Old English, from Owen, meaning 'well born' or 'noble'.

Ezra
Hebrew, meaning 'helper'. Associated with the poet Ezra Pound.

F

Boys' names

Faber
(alt. Fabir)
Latin, meaning 'blacksmith'.

Fabian
(alt. Fabien, Fabio)
Latin, meaning 'one who grows beans'.

Fabrice
(alt. Fabrizio)
Latin, meaning 'works with his hands'.

Faisal
Arabic, meaning 'resolute'.

Falco
(alt. Falcon, Falconer, Falke)
Latin, meaning 'falconer'.

Faron
Spanish, meaning 'pharaoh'.

Farrell
Gaelic, meaning 'hero'.

Faulkner
Latin, from 'falcon'.

Faustino
Latin, meaning 'fortunate'.

Fela
(alt. Felah, Fella, Fellah)
African, meaning 'a man who is warlike'. The name of the famous Nigerian musician Fela Kuti.

F

Names of poets

Andrew (Marvell)
Geoffrey (Chaucer)
Hugo (Williams)
John (Donne, Keats, Milton)
Percy (Bysshe Shelley)
Robert (Burns)
Siegfried (Sassoon)
Ted (Hughes)
Walt (Whitman)
William (Blake, Wordsworth)

Felipe
(alt. Filippo)
Spanish, meaning 'lover of horses'.

Felix
(alt. Felice)
Italian/Latin, meaning 'happy'.

Fennel
Latin, name of a herb.

Ferdinand
(alt. Fernando)
Old German, meaning 'bold voyager'.

Fergus
(alt. Ferguson)
Gaelic, meaning 'supreme man'.

Ferris
Gaelic, meaning 'rock'.

Fiachra
Irish, meaning 'raven'.

Fidel
Latin, meaning 'faithful'.

Finbar
Gaelic, meaning 'fair head'.

F

Finian
Gaelic, meaning 'fair'.

Finlay
(alt. Finley, Finn)
Gaelic, meaning 'fair haired courageous one'.

Finnegan
Gaelic, meaning 'fair'.

Fintan
Gaelic, meaning 'little fair one'.

Fitzroy
English, meaning 'the king's son'.

Flavio
Latin, meaning 'yellow hair'.

Florencio
(alt. Florentino)
Latin, meaning 'from Florence'.

Florian
(alt. Florin)
Slavic/Latin, meaning 'flower'.

Floyd
Welsh, meaning 'grey haired'.

Flynn
Gaelic, meaning 'with a ruddy complexion'.

Forbes
(alt. Forbs, Forb, Forbe)
Gaelic, meaning 'of the field'.

Fortunato
Italian, meaning 'lucky'.

Foster
Old English, meaning 'woodsman'.

Fotini
(alt. Fotis)
Greek, meaning 'light'.

Francesco
(alt. Francis, Francisco, Franco, François)
Latin, meaning 'from France'.

Frank
(alt. Frankie, Franklin, Franz)
Middle English, meaning 'free landholder'.

F

Fraser
Scottish, meaning 'of the forest men'.

Frederick
(alt. Freddie, Fred)
Old German, meaning 'peaceful ruler'.

Furman
Old German, meaning 'ferryman'.

Fyfe
(alt. Fife, Fyffes)
Scottish, meaning 'from Fifeshire'.

Boys' names

Gabe

Hebrew, shortened form of Gabriel, meaning 'hero of God'.

Gabino

Latin, meaning 'God is my strength'.

Gabriel

Hebrew, meaning 'hero of God'. One of the archangels.

Gael

English, old reference to the Celts.

Gaius

(alt. Gaeus)

Latin, meaning 'rejoicing'.

Galen

Greek, meaning 'healer'.

Galileo

Italian, meaning 'from Galilee'.

Ganesh

Hindi, meaning 'Lord of the throngs'. One of the Hindu deities.

Gannon

Irish, meaning 'fair skinned'.

Gareth

(alt. Garth)

Welsh, meaning 'gentle'.

Garfield

Old English, meaning 'spear field'. Also the name of the cartoon cat.

G

Garland
English, as in 'garland of flowers'.

Garnet
English, precious stone red in colour.

Garrett
Old German, meaning 'spear' or 'ruler'.

Garth
(alt. Garthe, Gart, Garte)
Norse, meaning 'enclosure'.

Gary
(alt. Garry, Geary)
Old English, meaning 'spear'.

Gaspar
(alt. Gaspard)
Persian, meaning 'treasurer'.

Gaston
From the Gascony region in the south of France.

Gavin
(alt. Gawain)
Scottish/Welsh, meaning 'little falcon'.

Gene
Greek, shortened form of Eugene, meaning 'well born'.

Genkei
Japanese, meaning 'honoured'.

Gennaro
Italian, meaning 'of Janus'.

Geoffrey
Old German, meaning 'peace'.

George
(alt. Giorgio)
Greek, meaning 'farmer'.

Gerald
(alt. Geraldo, Gerard, Gerardo, Gerhard)
Old German, meaning 'spear ruler'.

Geronimo
Italian, meaning 'sacred name'.

Gerry
English, meaning 'independent'.

G

Gert
Old German, meaning 'strong spear'.

Gervase
Old German, meaning 'with honour'.

Giacomo
Italian, meaning 'God's son'.

Gibson
English, meaning 'son of Gilbert'.

Gideon
Hebrew, meaning 'tree cutter'.

Gilbert
(alt. Gilberto)
French, meaning 'bright promise'.

Giles
Greek, meaning 'small goat'.

Gino
Italian, meaning 'well born'.

Giovanni
Italian form of John, meaning 'God is gracious'.

Giri
(alt. Gririe, Giry, Girey)
Indian, meaning 'from the mountain'.

Giulio
Italian, meaning 'youthful'.

Giuseppe
Italian form of Joseph, meaning 'Jehovah increases'.

Glen
English, from the word 'glen'.

Glyn
Welsh form of Glen.

Godfrey
German, meaning 'peace of God'.

Gordon
Gaelic, meaning 'large fortification'.

Gottlieb
German, meaning 'good love'.

Gower
Area on the Welsh coast.

G

Graeme
(alt. Graham)
English, meaning 'gravelled area'.

Grant
English, from the word 'grant'.

Granville
English, meaning 'gravelly town'.

Gray
(alt. Grey)
English, from the word 'gray'.

Grayson
English, meaning 'son of gray'.

Green
English, from the word 'green'.

Greg
(alt. Gregorio, Gregory, Grieg)
English, meaning 'watcher'.

Griffin
English, from the word 'griffin'.

Groves
English, meaning 'inhabits near grove of trees'.

Guido
Italian, meaning 'guide'.

Guillaume
French form of William, meaning 'strong protector'.

Gulliver
English, meaning 'glutton'.

Gunther
German, meaning 'warrior'.

Gurpreet
Indian, meaning 'love of the teacher'.

Gustave
(alt. Gus)
Scandinavian, meaning 'royal staff'.

Guy
English, from the word 'guy'.

Grylfi
(alt. Gylfie, Gylfee, Gylffi)
Scandinavian, meaning 'king'.

Gwyn
Welsh, meaning 'white'.

Boys' names

Habib
Arabic, meaning 'beloved one'.

Hackett
(alt. Hacket, Hackit, Hackitt)
German, meaning 'small hacker'.

Haden
(alt. Haiden)
English, meaning 'hedged valley'.

Hades
Greek, meaning 'sightless'. Name of the underworld in Greek mythology.

Hadrian
From Hadria, a north Italian city.

Hadwin
Old English, meaning 'friend in war'.

Hakeem
Arabic, meaning 'wise and insightful'.

Hal
(alt. Hale, Hallie)
English, nickname for Henry, meaning 'home ruler'.

Halim
Arabic, meaning 'gentle'.

Hallam
Old English, meaning 'the valley'.

Hamid
Arabic, meaning 'praiseworthy'.

H

Hamilton
Old English, meaning 'flat topped hill'.

Hamish
Scottish form of James, meaning 'he who supplants'.

Hamlet
(alt. Hamlett, Hammet, Hamnet)
German, meaning 'village'. A variation of the Danish Amleth, and often associated with Shakespeare's tragedy *Hamlet*.

Hampus
Swedish form of Homer, meaning 'pledge'.

Hamza
Arabic, meaning 'lamb'.

Han
(alt. Hannes, Hans)
Scandinavian, meaning 'the Lord is gracious'.

Hanif
(alt. Haneef, Haneaf, Haneif)
Arabic, meaning 'devout'.

Hank
German, meaning 'home ruler'. Form of Henry.

Hansel
German, meaning 'the Lord is gracious'.

Hardy
English, meaning 'tough'. Often associated with the author Thomas Hardy.

Harlan
English, meaning 'dweller by the boundary wood'.

Names from ancient Greece

Aeschylus
Erasmus
Hieronymus
Homer
Jason
Leonidas
Nikolaos
Sophocles
Theodore

H

Harland

Old English, meaning 'army land'.

Harley

Old English, meaning 'hare meadow'.

Harmon

Old German, meaning 'soldier'.

Harold

Scandinavian, meaning 'army ruler'.

Harry

Old German, meaning 'home ruler'. Form of Henry.

Hart

Old English, meaning 'stag'.

Harvey

Old English, meaning 'strong and worthy'.

Haskell

Hebrew, meaning 'intellect'.

Hassan

Arabic, meaning 'handsome'.

Haydn

(alt. Hayden, Haydon)

Old English, meaning 'hedged valley'.

Heart

English, from the word 'heart'.

Heath

English, meaning 'heath' or 'moor'.

Heathcliff

English, meaning 'cliff near a heath'. Made famous by Emily Bronte's novel *Wuthering Heights*.

Heber

Hebrew, meaning 'partner'.

Hector

Greek, meaning 'steadfast'.

Henry

(alt. Henri, Hendrik, Hendrix)

Old German, meaning 'home ruler'.

Henson

English, meaning 'son of Henry'.

H

Herbert
(alt. Bert, Herb)
Old German, meaning 'illustrious warrior'.

Heriberto
Spanish variant of Herbert, meaning 'illustrious warrior'.

Herman
(alt. Herminio, Hermon)
Old German, meaning 'soldier'.

Hermes
Greek, meaning 'messenger'. The messenger of the gods in Greek mythology.

Herschel
Yiddish, meaning 'deer'.

Hezekiah
Hebrew, meaning 'God gives strength'.

Hideki
Japanese, meaning 'excellent trees'.

Hideo
Japanese, meaning 'excellent name'.

Hilario
Latin, meaning 'cheerful, happy'.

Hilary
English, meaning 'cheerful'.

Hillel
Hebrew, meaning 'greatly praised'.

Hilliard
Old German, meaning 'battle guard'.

Hilton
Old English, meaning 'hill settlement'.

Hiram
Hebrew, meaning 'exalted brother'.

Hiro
Spanish, meaning 'sacred name'.

Hiroshi
Japanese, meaning 'generous'.

Hirsch
Yiddish, meaning 'deer'.

H

Hobart

English, meaning 'bright and shining intellect'.

Hodge

English, meaning 'son of Roger'.

Hogan

Gaelic, meaning 'youth'.

Holden

English, meaning 'deep valley'.

Hollis

Old English, meaning 'holly tree'.

Homer

Greek, meaning 'pledge'. Name of the Greek poet, and the TV character Homer Simpson.

Honorius

Latin, meaning 'honourable'.

Horace

Latin, name of the Roman poet.

Houston

Old English, meaning 'Hugh's town'. Also a city in the state of Texas, USA.

Howard

Old English, meaning 'noble watchman'.

Howell

Welsh, meaning 'eminent and remarkable'.

Hoyt

Norse, meaning 'spirit' or 'soul'.

Hristo

From Christo, meaning 'follower of Christ'.

Hubbell

(alt. Hubble)

English, meaning 'brave hearted'.

Hubert

German, meaning 'bright and shining intellect'.

Hudson

Old English, meaning 'son of Hugh'.

Hugh

Old German, meaning 'soul, mind and intellect'.

H

Hugo

German, meaning 'bright in mind and spirit'.

Humbert

Old German, meaning 'famous giant'. Be warned: it's the name and surname of the paedophile protagonist of Vladimir Nabokov's *Lolita*.

Humphrey

Old German, meaning 'peaceful warrior'.

Hunter

English, from the word 'hunter'.

Hurley

Gaelic, meaning 'sea tide'.

Huxley

Old English, meaning 'Hugh's meadow'.

Hyrum

Hebrew, meaning 'exalted brother'.

Surnames as first names

Campbell
Connor
Cooper
Hamilton
Harrison

Lewis
Jackson
Taylor
Walker
Watson

Boys' names

Iago

Spanish, meaning 'he who supplants'. Name of the villain in Shakespeare's *Othello*.

Ian
(alt. Ion)

Gaelic, variant of John, meaning 'God is gracious'.

Ianto

Welsh, meaning 'gift of God'.

Ibaad

Arabic, meaning 'a believer in God'.

Ibrahim

Arabic, meaning 'father of many'.

Ichabod

Hebrew, meaning 'glory is good'.

Ichiro

Japanese, meaning 'firstborn son'.

Idan

Hebrew, meaning 'place in time'.

Idris

Welsh, meaning 'fiery leader'.

Ifan

Welsh variant of John, meaning 'God is gracious'.

I

Ignacio
Latin, meaning 'ardent' or 'burning'.

Ignatz
German, meaning 'fiery'.

Igor
Russian, meaning 'Ing's soldier'.

Ikaika
Hawaiian, meaning 'strong'.

Ike
Hebrew, short for Isaac, meaning 'laughter'.

Iku
Japanese, meaning 'nourishing'.

Ilan
Hebrew, meaning 'tree'.

Ilias
Variant of Hebrew Elijah, meaning 'the Lord is my God'.

Imanol
Hebrew, meaning 'God is with us'.

Indiana
Latin, meaning 'from India'. Also a state in the USA.

Indigo
English, describing a deep blue colour.

Ingo
Danish, meaning 'meadow'.

Inigo
Spanish, meaning 'fiery'.

Ioannis
Greek, meaning 'the Lord is gracious'.

Girls' names for boys (male spellings)

Darcy
Gene (or Jean in France)
Kay
Kelly
Kelsey
Madison
Nat
Paris
Sandy
Sasha

Iovianno

Native American, meaning
'yellow hawk'.

Ira

Hebrew, meaning 'full grown
and watchful'.

Irvin

(alt. Irving, Irwin)

Gaelic, meaning 'green and
fresh water'.

Isaac

(alt. Isaak)

Hebrew, meaning 'laughter'.

Isadore

(alt. Isidore, Isidro)

Greek, meaning 'gift of Isis'.

Isai

(alt. Isaiah, Isaias, Izaiah)

Arabic, meaning 'protection
and security'.

Iser

Yiddish, meaning 'God
wrestler'.

Ishedus

Native American, meaning 'on
top'.

Place names

Austin
Carson
Chester
Glen
Jericho
London
Paris
Seymour
Whitley
Windsor

Ishmael

(alt. Ismael)

Hebrew, meaning 'God listens'.

Israel

Hebrew, meaning 'God
perseveres'. Also the name of
the country.

Istvan

Hungarian variant of Stephen,
meaning 'crowned'.

Itai

Hebrew, meaning 'the Lord is
with me'.

I

Ivan

Hebrew, meaning 'God is gracious'.

Ivanhoe

Russian, meaning 'God is gracious'. Also name of the novel by Walter Scott.

Ivey

English, variant of Ivy.

Ivo

French, from the word 'yves', meaning 'yew tree'.

Ivor

Scandinavian, meaning 'yew'.

Ivory

English, from the word 'ivory'.

Izar

Basque, meaning 'star'.

J Boys' names

Jabari
Swahili, meaning 'valiant'.

Jabez
Hebrew, meaning 'borne in pain'.

Jabulani
(alt. Jabulanie, Jabulany, Jabulaney)
African, meaning 'happy one'.

Jace
(alt. Jaece, Jase, Jayce)
Hebrew, meaning 'healer'.

Jacek
African, meaning 'hyacinth'.

Jacinto
African, meaning 'hyacinth'.

Jack
(alt. Jackie, Jacky)
From the Hebrew John, meaning 'God is gracious'. The UK's most popular boy's name for 14 years until 2011.

Jackson
English, meaning 'son of Jack'.

Jaco
Hebrew, from Jacob, meaning 'he who supplants'.

Jacob
(alt. Jacobo, Jago)
Hebrew, meaning 'he who supplants'.

Jacques
French form of Jack, meaning 'God is gracious'.

Jaden
(alt. Jaden, Jadyn, Jaeden, Jaiden, Jaidyn, Jayden, Jaydin)
Hebrew, meaning 'Jehovah has heard'.

Jaegar
(alt. Jager, Jaecer, Jaegar)
German, meaning 'mighty hunter'.

Jafar
Arabic, meaning 'stream'.

Jagger
Old English, meaning 'one who cuts'.

Jaheem
(alt. Jaheim)
Hebrew, meaning 'raised up'.

Jahir
Hindi, meaning 'jewel'.

Jaime
Variant of James, meaning 'he who supplants'. 'J'aime' is French for 'I love'.

Jair
(alt. Jairo)
Hebrew, meaning 'God enlightens'.

Jake
Shortened form of Jacob, meaning 'he who supplants'.

Jalen
Greek, meaning 'healer' or 'tranquil'.

Jali
Swahili, meaning 'musician'.

Jalon
Greek, meaning 'healer' or 'tranquil'.

Jamaal
(alt. Jamal)
Arabic, meaning 'handsome'.

Jamar
(alt. Jamarcus, Jamari, Jamarion, Jamir)
Modern variant of Jamaal, meaning 'handsome'.

Jamel
Arabic, meaning 'handsome'.

J

James
English, meaning 'he who supplants'.

Jameson
(alt. Jamison)
English, meaning 'son of James'.

Jamie
(alt. Jamey, Jaimie)
Nickname for James, meaning 'he who supplants'.

Jamil
Arabic, meaning 'handsome'.

Jamin
Hebrew, meaning 'son of the right hand'.

Jan
(alt. Janko, János)
Slavic, from John, meaning 'the Lord is gracious'.

Janesh
Hindi, meaning 'leader of people'.

Janus
Latin, meaning 'gateway'. Roman god of doors, beginnings and endings.

Japhet
(alt. Japheth)
Hebrew, meaning 'comely'.

Jaquez
French, form of Jacques, meaning 'God is gracious'.

Jared
(alt. Jarem, Jaren, Jaret, Jarod, Jarrod)
Hebrew, meaning 'descending'.

Short names

Al
Ben
Dev
Ed
Jo
Kev
Max
Rob
Sam
Ty

J

Jarlath
Gaelic, from Iarlaith, from Saint Iarfhlaith.

Jarom
Greek, meaning 'to raise and exalt'.

Jarrell
Variant of Gerald, meaning 'spear ruler'.

Jarrett
Old English, meaning 'spear-brave'.

Jarvis
Old German, meaning 'with honour'.

Jason
Greek, meaning 'healer'.

Jasper
Greek, meaning 'treasure holder'.

Javen
Arabic, meaning 'youth'.

Javier
Spanish, meaning 'bright'.

Jaxon
From Jackson, meaning 'son of Jack'.

Jay
Latin, meaning 'jaybird'.

Jaylan
Greek, meaning 'healer'.

Jeevan
Indian, meaning 'life'.

Jeffrey
(alt. Jeff)
Old German, meaning 'peace'.

Jefferson
English, meaning 'son of Jeffrey'.

Jensen
Scandinavian, meaning 'son of Jan'.

Jeremiah
(alt. Jeremia, Jeremias, Jeremiya)
Hebrew, meaning 'the Lord exalts'.

J

Jeremy
(alt. Jem)
Hebrew, meaning 'the Lord exalts'.

Jeriah
Hebrew, meaning 'Jehovah has seen'.

Jericho
Arabic, meaning 'city of the moon'.

Jermaine
Latin, meaning 'brotherly'.

Jerome
Greek, meaning 'sacred name'.

Jerry
English, from Gerald, meaning 'spear ruler'.

Jesse
Hebrew, meaning 'the Lord exists'.

Jesus
Hebrew, meaning 'the Lord is Salvation' and the Son of God.

Jethro
Hebrew, meaning 'eminent'.

Jignesh
(alt. Jigneshe, Jygnesh, Jygneshe)
Indian, meaning 'curious'.

Jim
(alt. Jimmy)
From James, meaning 'he who supplants'.

Jiri
(alt. Jiro)
Greek, meaning 'farmer'.

Joachim
Hebrew, meaning 'established by God'.

Joah
(alt. João)
Hebrew, meaning 'God is gracious'.

Joaquin
Hebrew, meaning 'established by God'. Made famous by the actor Joaquin Phoenix.

J

Joe
(alt. Joey, Johan, Johannes, Jomar)
From Joseph, meaning 'Jehovah increases'.

Joel
Hebrew, meaning 'Jehovah is the Lord'.

John
Hebrew, meaning 'God is gracious'.

Johnny
(alt. Jon, Jonny)
From Jonathan, meaning 'gift of God'.

Jolyon
From Julian, meaning 'young'.

Jonah
Hebrew, meaning 'dove'.

Jonas
Hebrew, meaning 'dove'.

Jonathan
(alt. Johnathan, Johnathon, Jonathon, Jonty)
Hebrew, meaning 'God is gracious'.

Jordan
(alt. Jory, Judd)
Hebrew, meaning 'down-flowing'.

Jorge
From George, meaning 'farmer'.

José
Spanish variant of Joseph, meaning 'God increases'.

Joseph
(alt. Joss)
Hebrew, meaning 'God increases'.

Josh
Shortened form of Joshua, meaning 'God is salvation'.

Joshua
Hebrew, meaning 'God is salvation'.

Josiah
Hebrew, meaning 'God helps'.

Josué
Spanish variant of Joshua, meaning 'God is salvation'.

J

'Bad boy' names

Arnie
Axel
Brett
Conan
Damian
Guy
Ivan
Preston
Stanley
Tyson

Jovan

Latin, meaning 'the supreme God'.

Joweese

Native American, meaning 'chirping bird'.

Joyce

Latin, meaning 'joy'.

Juan

Spanish variant of John, meaning 'God is gracious'.

Jubal

Hebrew, meaning 'ram's horn'.

Jude

Hebrew, meaning 'praise' or 'thanks'. The title character in Hardy's novel *Jude the Obscure*.

Judson

Variant of Jude, meaning 'praise' or 'thanks'.

Jules

From Julian, meaning 'Jove's child'.

Julian

Greek, meaning 'Jove's child'.

Julien

French variant of Julian, meaning 'Jove's child'.

Julio

Spanish variant of Julian, meaning 'Jove's child'.

Julius

Latin, meaning 'youthful'.

Junior

Latin, meaning 'the younger one'.

J

Junius

Latin, meaning 'young'.

Jupiter

Latin, meaning 'the supreme God'. Jupiter was king of the Roman gods and the god of thunder. Jupiter is also the largest planet in the solar system.

Juraj

Hebrew, meaning 'God is my judge'.

Jurgen

Greek, meaning 'farmer'.

Justice

English, from the word 'justice'.

Justin
(alt. Justus)

Latin, meaning 'just and upright'.

Juwan

Hebrew, meaning 'the Lord is gracious'.

Famous male drummers

Dave (Grohl)
John (Bonham)
Keith (Moon)
Lars (Ulrich)
Mick (Fleetwood)

Phil (Collins)
Ringo (Starr)
Stewart (Copeland)
Tommy (Lee)
Travis (Barker)

K Boys' names

Kaamil

Arabic, meaning 'perfect'.

Kabelo

African, meaning 'gift'.

Kade

Scottish, meaning 'from the wetlands'.

Kadeem

Arabic, meaning 'one who serves'.

Kaden

(alt. Kadin, Kaeden, Kaedin, Kaiden)

Arabic, meaning 'companion'.

Kadir

Arabic, meaning 'capable and competent'.

Kafka

Czech, meaning 'bird-like'. Often associated with the author of *The Metamorphosis*.

Kahlil

Arabic, meaning 'friend'.

Kai

Greek, meaning 'keeper of the keys'.

Kaito

Japanese, meaning 'ocean and sake dipper'.

K

Kalani
Hawaiian, meaning 'sky'.

Kale
German, meaning 'free man'.

Kaleb
(alt. Caleb)
Hebrew, meaning 'dog' or 'aggressive'.

Kalen
Gaelic, meaning 'uncertain'.

Kaleo
Hawaiian, meaning 'the voice'.

Kalil
Arabic, meaning 'friend'.

Kalvin
French, meaning 'bald'.

Kamari
Indian, meaning 'the enemy of desire'.

Kamden
English, meaning 'winding valley'.

Kamil
Arabic, meaning 'perfection'.

Kane
Gaelic, meaning 'little battler'.

Kani
Hawaiian, meaning 'sound'.

Kanye
African town. Made popular by rapper Kanye West.

Kareem
(alt. Karim)
Arabic, meaning 'generous'.

Karl
(alt. Karson)
Old German, meaning 'free man'.

Kasey
Irish, meaning 'alert'.

Kaspar
Persian, meaning 'treasurer'.

Kavon
Gaelic, meaning 'handsome'.

K

Kayden

Arabic, meaning 'companion'.

Kazimierz

Polish, meaning 'declares peace'.

Kazuki

Japanese, meaning 'radiant hope'.

Kazuo

Japanese, meaning 'harmonious man'.

Keagan
(alt. Keegan, Kegan)

Gaelic, meaning 'small flame'.

Keane

Gaelic, meaning 'fighter'.

Keanu

Hawaiian, meaning 'breeze'. Made famous by the actor Keanu Reeves.

Keary

Gaelic, meaning 'black-haired'.

Keaton

English, meaning 'place of hawks'.

Keefe
(alt. Keef, Kief, Kiefe)

Gaelic, meaning 'beautiful and graceful'.

Keeler

Gaelic, meaning 'beautiful and graceful'.

Keenan
(alt. Kenan)

Gaelic, meaning 'little ancient one'.

Keiji

Japanese, meaning 'govern with discretion'.

Keir

Gaelic, meaning 'dark-haired' or 'dark-skinned'.

Keith

Gaelic, meaning 'woodland'.

Kekoa

Hawaiian, meaning 'brave one' or 'soldier'.

Kelby

Old English, meaning 'farmhouse near the stream'.

K

Kell

(alt. Kellan, Kellen, Kelley, Kelly, Kiel)

Norse, meaning 'spring'.

Kelsey

Old English, meaning 'victorious ship'.

Kelton

Old English, meaning 'town of the keels'.

Kelvin

Old English, meaning 'friend of ships'.

Kemenes

Hungarian, meaning 'maker of furnaces'.

Ken

Shortened form of Kenneth, meaning 'born of fire'.

Kendal

Old English, meaning 'the Kent river valley'.

Kendon

Old English, meaning 'brave guard'.

Kendrick

Gaelic, meaning 'royal ruler'.

Kenelm

Old English, meaning 'bold'.

Kenji

Japanese, meaning 'intelligent second son'.

Kennedy

Gaelic, meaning 'helmet head'.

Kenneth

(alt. Kenney)

Gaelic, meaning 'born of fire'.

Kennison

English, meaning 'son of Kenneth'.

Kent

From the English county.

Kenton

English, meaning 'town of Ken'.

Kenya

From the country in Africa.

Kenzo

Japanese, meaning 'wise'.

K

Keola
Hawaiian, meaning 'life'.

Keon
(alt. Keoni)
Hawaiian, meaning 'gracious'.

Kepler
German, meaning 'hat maker'.

Kermit
(alt. Kerwin)
Gaelic, meaning 'without envy'. Associated with Kermit the Frog, the Muppets character.

Kerr
English, meaning 'wetland'.

Keshav
Indian, meaning 'beautiful-haired'.

Kevin
Gaelic, meaning 'handsome beloved'.

Khalid
(alt. Khalif, Khalil)
Arabic, meaning 'immortal'.

Kian
(alt. Keyon, Kyan)
Irish, meaning 'ancient'.

Kiefer
German, meaning 'barrel maker'.

Kieran
(alt. Kyron)
Gaelic, meaning 'black'.

Kijana
African, meaning 'youth'.

Kilby
From the English 'Cilebi', a place in Leicestershire.

Kilian
Irish, meaning 'bright headed'.

Kimani
African, meaning 'beautiful and sweet'.

King
English, from the word 'king'.

Kingsley
English, meaning 'the king's meadow'.

Kirby

German, meaning 'settlement by a church'.

Kirk

Old German, meaning 'church'.

Klaus

German, meaning 'victorious'.

Knightley
(alt. Knightly)

English, meaning 'of the knight's meadows'. Surname of the hero in Jane Austen's *Emma*.

Kobe
(alt. Koda, Kody)

Japanese, meaning 'a Japanese city'.

Kofi

Ghanaian, meaning 'born on Friday'.

Kohana

Japanese, meaning 'little flower'.

Kojo

Ghanaian, meaning 'Monday'.

Kolby

Norse, meaning 'settlement'.

Korbin

Gaelic, meaning 'a steep hill'.

Kramer

German, meaning 'shopkeeper'.

Kris
(alt. Krish)

From Christopher, meaning 'bearing Christ inside'.

Kurt

German, meaning 'courageous advice'.

Kurtis

French, meaning 'courtier'.

Kwame

Ghanaian, meaning 'born on Saturday'.

Kyden

English, meaning 'narrow little fire'.

Kylan
(alt. Kyle, Kyleb, Kyler)

Gaelic, meaning 'narrow and straight'.

Kyllion

Irish, meaning 'war'.

Kyree

From Cree, a Canadian tribe.

Kyros

Greek, meaning 'legitimate power'.

English and Scottish royalty

Alexander	James
Charles	Richard
Edward	Robert
George	Stephen
Henry	William

Literary names

Charlie (*Charlie and the Chocolate Factory*, Roald Dahl)

Christopher (*Now We Are Six*, A. A. Milne)

David (*David Copperfield*, Charles Dickens)

Gabriel (*Far from the Madding Crowd*, Thomas Hardy)

Dorian (*The Picture of Dorian Gray*, Oscar Wilde)

Ishmael (*Moby Dick*, Herman Melville)

James (*James and the Giant Peach*, Roald Dahl)

Karin (*The Buddha of Suburbia*, Hanif Kureishi)

Phileas (*Around the World in Eighty Days*, Jules Verne)

Richard (*The Beach*, Alex Garland)

Winston (*Nineteen Eighty-Four*, George Orwell)

L Boys' names

Laban
Hebrew, meaning 'white'.

Lachlan
Gaelic, meaning 'from the land of lakes'.

Lacy
Old French, after the place in France.

Laertes
English, meaning 'adventurous'. Ophelia's brother in Shakespeare's *Hamlet*.

Lalit
Hindi, meaning 'beautiful'.

Lamar
Old German, meaning 'water'.

Lambert
Scandinavian, meaning 'land brilliant'.

Lambros
Greek, meaning 'brilliant and radiant'.

Lamont
Old Norse, meaning 'law man'.

Lance
French, meaning 'land'.

Lancelot
Variant of Lance, meaning 'land'. The name of one of the Knights of the Round Table.

Landen
(*alt. Lando, Landon, Langdon*)
English, meaning 'long hill'.

L

Landyn

Welsh variant of Landen, meaning 'long hill'.

Lane
(alt. Layne)

English, from the word 'lanel'.

Lang

Norse, meaning 'long meadow'.

Lannie
(alt. Lanny)

German, meaning 'precious'.

Larkin

Gaelic, meaning 'rough' or 'fierce'.

Laron

French, meaning 'thief'.

Larry

Latin, variant of Lawrence, meaning 'man from Laurentum'.

Lars

Scandinavian variant of Lawrence, meaning 'man from Laurentum'.

Lasse

Finnish, meaning 'girl'. (Still, ironically, a boy's name.)

Laszlo

Hungarian, meaning 'glorious rule'.

Lathyn

Latin, meaning 'fighter'.

Latif

Arabic, meaning 'gentle'.

Laurel

Latin, meaning 'bay'.

Laurent

French form of Lawrence, meaning 'man from Laurentum'.

Lawrence

Latin, meaning 'man from Laurentum'.

Lazarus

Hebrew, meaning 'God is my help'.

Leandro

Latin, meaning 'lion man'.

Lear

German, meaning 'of the meadow'.

Lee
(alt. Leigh)

Old English, meaning 'meadow' or 'valley'.

Leib

German, meaning 'love'.

Leif

Scandinavian, meaning 'heir'.

Leith

From the name of a place in Scotland.

Lennox
(alt. Lenny)

Gaelic, meaning 'with many elm trees'.

Leo

Latin, meaning 'lion'.

Leon

Latin, meaning 'lion'.

Leonard

Old German, meaning 'lion strength'.

Leopold

German, meaning 'brave people'.

Leroy

French, meaning 'king'.

Lesley
(alt. Les)

Scottish, meaning 'holly garden'.

Lester

English, meaning 'from Leicester'.

Lewis

French, meaning 'renowned fighter'.

Lex

English variant of Alexander, meaning 'defending men'.

Liam

German, meaning 'helmet'.

Lincoln

English, meaning 'lake colony'.

L

Lindsay
Scottish, meaning 'linden tree'.

Linus
Latin, meaning 'lion'.

Lionel
English, meaning 'lion'.

Llewellyn
Welsh, meaning 'like a lion'.

Lloyd
Welsh, meaning 'grey-haired and sacred'.

Logan
Gaelic, meaning 'hollow'.

Lonnie
English, meaning 'lion strength'.

Lorcan
Gaelic, meaning 'little fierce one'.

Louis
(alt. Lou, Louie, Luigi, Luis)
German, meaning 'famous warrior'.

Lucas
(alt. Lukas)
English, meaning 'man from Luciana'.

Lucian
(alt. Lucio)
Latin, meaning 'light'.

Ludwig
German, meaning 'famous fighter'.

Luke
(alt. Luc, Luka)
Latin, meaning 'from Lucanus'.

Lupe
Latin, meaning 'wolf'.

Luther
German, meaning 'soldier of the people'.

Lyle
French, meaning 'the island'.

Lyn
(alt. Lyndon)
Spanish, meaning 'pretty'.

M Boys' names

Mabon
(alt. Maban, Mabery)
Welsh, meaning 'our son'.

Mac
(alt. Mack, Mackie)
Scottish, meaning 'son of'.

Macaulay
Scottish, meaning 'son of the phantom'.

Mace
English, meaning 'heavy staff' or 'club'.

Mackenzie
Scottish, meaning 'the fair one'.

Mackland
Scottish, meaning 'land of Mac'.

Macon
French, name of towns in France and Georgia.

Macsen
Scottish, meaning 'son of Mac'.

Madden
Irish, meaning 'descendant of the hound'.

Maddox
English, meaning 'good' or 'generous'.

Madison
(alt. Madsen)
Irish, meaning 'son of Madden'.

M

Mads
Shortened form of Madden, meaning 'descendant of the hound'.

Magnus
(alt. Manus)
Latin, meaning 'great'.

Maguire
Gaelic, meaning 'son of the beige one'.

Mahabala
Indian, meaning 'great strength'.

Mahesh
Hindi, meaning 'great ruler'.

Mahir
Arabic, meaning 'skilful'.

Mahlon
Hebrew, meaning 'sickness'.

Mahmoud
Arabic, meaning 'praiseworthy'.

Mahoney
Irish, meaning 'bear'.

Major
English, from the word 'major'.

Makal
From Michael, meaning 'close to God'.

Makani
Hawaiian, meaning 'wind'.

Makis
Hebrew, meaning 'gift from God'.

Mako
Hebrew, meaning 'God is with us'.

Malachi
(alt. Malachy)
Irish, meaning 'messenger of God'.

Malcolm
English, meaning 'Columba's servant'.

Mali
Arabic, meaning 'full and rich'.

Manfred
Old German, meaning 'man of peace'.

Manish
English, meaning 'manly'.

Manley
English, meaning 'manly and brave'.

Mannix
Gaelic, meaning 'little monk'.

Manoi
(alt. Manos)
Japanese, meaning 'love springing from intellect'.

Manuel
Hebrew, meaning 'God is with us'.

Manzi
Italian, meaning 'steer'.

Marc
(alt. Marco, Marcos, Marcus, Markel)
French, meaning 'from the god Mars'.

Marcel
(alt. Marcelino, Marcello)
French, meaning 'little warrior'.

Marek
Polish variant of Mark, meaning 'from the god Mars'.

Mariano
Latin, meaning 'from the god Mars'.

Mario
(alt. Marius)
Latin, meaning 'manly'.

Mark
English, meaning 'from the god Mars'.

Marley
(alt. Marlin)
Old English, meaning 'meadow near the lake'.

Marlon
English, meaning 'like little hawk'. Famous as the forename of Marlon Brando.

Marshall
Old French, meaning 'caretaker of horses'.

Martin
Latin, meaning 'dedicated to Mars'.

M

Marty
Shortened form of Martin, meaning 'dedicated to Mars'.

Marvel
English, from the word 'marvel'.

Marvin
Welsh, meaning 'sea friend'.

Mason
English, from the word 'mason'.

Massimo
Italian, meaning 'greatest'.

Mathias
(alt. Matthias)
Hebrew, meaning 'gift of the Lord'.

Mathieu
French form of Matthew, meaning 'gift of God'.

Matthew
Hebrew, meaning 'gift of the Lord'.

Maurice
(alt. Mauricio)
Latin, meaning 'dark skinned' or 'Moorish'.

Maverick
American, meaning 'non-conformist leader'.

Max
(alt. Maxie, Maxim)
Latin, meaning 'greatest'.

Maximillian
Latin, meaning 'greatest'.

Maximino
Latin, meaning 'little Max'.

Maxwell
Latin, meaning 'Maccus' stream'.

Maynard
Old German, meaning 'brave'.

McArthur
Scottish, meaning 'son of Arthur'.

McCoy
Scottish, meaning 'son of Coy'.

Mearl
English, meaning 'my earl'.

Mederic
French, meaning 'doctor'.

Mekhi
African, meaning 'who is God?'.

Mel
Gaelic, meaning 'smooth brow'.

Melbourne
From the city in Australia.

Melchior
Persian, meaning 'king of the city'.

Melton
English, meaning 'town of Mel'.

Melva
Hawaiian, meaning 'plumeria'.

Melville
Scottish, meaning 'town of Mel'.

Melvin
(alt. Melvyn)
English, meaning 'smooth brow'.

Memphis
Greek, meaning 'established and beautiful'. Also the name of a city in the USA.

Mercer
English, from the word 'mercer'.

Merl
French, meaning 'blackbird'.

Merlin
Welsh, meaning 'sea fortress'.

Merrick
Welsh, meaning 'Moorish'.

Merrill
Gaelic, meaning 'shining sea'.

Merritt
English, from the word 'merit'.

Merton
Old English, meaning 'town by the lake'.

Meyer
Hebrew, meaning 'bright farmer'.

Michael

Hebrew, meaning 'resembles God'. One of the archangels.

Michalis

Greek form of Michael, meaning 'resembles God'.

Michel

French form of Michael, meaning 'resembles God'.

Michelangelo

Italian, meaning 'Michael's angel'. Name of the famous painter.

Michele

Italian form of Michael, meaning 'resembles God'.

Michio

Japanese, meaning 'a man with the strength of three thousand men'.

Mickey

Variant of Michael meaning 'resembles God'. Often associated with the Disney character Mickey Mouse.

Miguel

Spanish form of Michael, meaning 'resembles God'.

Mike

Shortened form of Michael, meaning 'resembles God'.

Miklos

Greek form of Michael, meaning 'resembles God'.

Milan

From the name of the Italian city.

Miles

(alt. Milo, Milos, Myles)
English, from the word 'miles'.

Milton

English, meaning 'miller's town'. Also the name of the poet John Milton.

Miro

Slavic, meaning 'peace'.

Misha

Russian, meaning 'who is like God'.

Football players

Aaron (Lennon)
Alan (Shearer)
Ashley (Cole)
David (Beckham)
Frank (Lampard)
Gary (Lineker)
Jack (Wilshere)
Joe (Cole)
John (Terry)
Rio (Ferdinand)
Scott (Parker)
Steven (Gerrard)
Wayne (Rooney)

Mitch
Shortened form of Mitchell, meaning 'who is like God'.

Mitchell
English, meaning 'who is like God'.

Modesto
Italian, meaning 'modest'.

Moe
Hebrew, meaning 'God's helmet'.

Mohamed
(alt. Mohammad, Mohamet, Mohammed)
Arabic, meaning 'praiseworthy'.

Monroe
Gaelic, meaning 'mouth of the river Rotha'.

Monserrate
Latin, meaning 'jagged mountain'.

Montague
French, meaning 'pointed hill'.

Montana
Latin, meaning 'mountain'. Also a state in the USA.

Monte
Italian, meaning 'mountain'.

Montgomery
Variant of Montague, meaning 'pointed hill'.

Monty
Shortened form of Montague, meaning 'pointed hill'.

M

Moody

English, from the word 'moody'.

Mordecai

Hebrew, meaning 'little man'.

Morgan

Welsh, meaning 'circling sea'.

Moritz

Latin, meaning 'dark skinned and Moorish'.

Morpheus

Greek, meaning 'shape'.

Morris

Welsh, meaning 'dark skinned and Moorish'.

Morrison

English, meaning 'son of Morris'.

Mortimer

French, meaning 'dead sea'.

Morton

Old English, meaning 'moor town'.

Moses

(alt. Moshe, Moshon)

Hebrew, meaning 'saviour'. In the Bible, Moses receives the Ten Commandments from God.

Moss

English, from the word 'moss'.

Muir

Gaelic, meaning 'of the moor'.

Mungo

Gaelic, meaning 'most dear'.

Murl

French, meaning 'blackbird'.

Murphy

Irish, meaning 'sea warrior'.

Murray

Gaelic, meaning 'lord and master'.

Mustafa

Arabic, meaning 'chosen'.

Myron

Greek, meaning 'myrrh'.

Mwita

African, meaning 'humourous one'.

# N

Boys' names

Nairn

Scottish, meaning 'alder-tree river'.

Najee

Arabic, meaning 'dear companion'.

Nakia

Arabic, meaning 'pure'.

Nakul

Indian, meaning 'mongoose'.

Naphtali

Hebrew, meaning 'wrestling'.

Napoleon

Italian, meaning 'man from Naples'. Name of the French general who became Emperor of France.

Narciso

Latin, from the myth of Narcissus, famous for drowning after falling in love with his own reflection.

Nash

English, meaning 'at the ash tree'.

Nasir

Arabic, meaning 'helper'.

N

Popular song names

Adam (*Adam's Son*, Blink 182)
Al (*You Can Call Me Al*, Paul Simon)
Alejandro (*Alejandro*, Lady Gaga)
Anthony (*Movin' Out*, Billy Joel)
Daniel (*Daniel*, Elton John)
Frankie (*Frankie*, Sister Sledge)
Jimmy (*Jimmy Mack*, Martha Reeves and the Vandellas)
Joe (*Hey Joe*, Jimi Hendrix)
Maxwell (*Maxwell's Silver Hammer*, The Beatles)
Robert (*Doctor Robert*, The Beatles)
William (*William It Was Really Nothing*, The Smiths)

Nate
Hebrew, meaning 'God has given'.

Nathan
(alt. Nathaniel)
Hebrew, meaning 'God has given'.

Naval
Indian, meaning 'wonder'.

Naveen
Indian, meaning 'new'.

Neal
Irish, meaning 'champion'.

Ned
Nickname for Edward, meaning 'wealthy guard'.

Neftali
Hebrew, meaning 'struggling'.

Nehemiah
Hebrew, meaning 'comforter'.

Neil
(alt. Niall)
Irish, meaning 'champion'.

Neilson
Irish, meaning 'son of Neil'.

Nelson
Variant of Neil, meaning 'champion'.

Nemo
Latin, meaning 'nobody'.

Neo
Latin, meaning 'new'.

Nephi
Greek, meaning 'cloud'.

Nessim
Arabic, meaning 'breeze'.

Nestor
Greek, meaning 'traveller'.

Neville
Old French, meaning 'new village'.

Newland
(alt. Newlands, Newland, Neuland)
English, meaning 'from a new land'.

Newton
English, meaning 'new town'.

Nicholas
(alt. Niklas)
Greek, meaning 'victorious'.

Nick
(alt. Niko, Nikos, Nico)
Shortened form of Nicholas, meaning 'victorious'.

Nigel
Gaelic, meaning 'champion'.

Nikhil
Hindi, meaning 'whole' or 'entire'.

Nikita
Greek, meaning 'unconquered'. Also a girl's name.

Nikolai
Russian variant of Nicholas, meaning 'victorious'.

Nimrod
Hebrew, meaning 'we will rebel'.

Ninian
Gaelic, associated with the 5th-century saint of the same name.

Nissim
Hebrew, meaning 'wonderful things'.

N

Noah
Hebrew, meaning 'peaceful'.

Noel
French, meaning 'Christmas'.

Nolan
Gaelic, meaning 'champion'.

Norbert
Old German, meaning 'Northern brightness'.

Norman
Old German, meaning 'Northerner'.

Normand
French, meaning 'from Normandy'.

Norris
Old French, meaning 'Northerner'.

Norton
English, meaning 'Northern town'.

Norval
French, meaning 'Northern town'.

Norwood
English, meaning 'Northern forest'.

Nova
Latin, meaning 'new'.

Nuno
Latin, meaning 'ninth'.

Nunzio
Italian, meaning 'messenger'.

Nyoka
African, meaning 'like a snake'.

Names of gods

Apollo (Music: Greek)
Eros (Love: Greek)
Hermes (Messenger of the gods)
Janus (Gates and Doors: Roman)
Mars (War: Roman)
Neptune (Sea: Roman)
Odin (Chief god: Norse)
Ra (Sun: Egyptian)
Thor (Thunder: Norse)

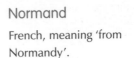

Boys' names

Oakley

English, meaning 'from the oak meadow'.

Obadiah

Hebrew, meaning 'God's worker'.

Obama

African, meaning 'crooked'. Made famous by the American President Barack Obama.

Obed

Hebrew, meaning 'servant of God'.

Popular French names

Alain	Jean
Alphonse	Louis
Gerard	Luc
Guy	Marc
Jacques	Mathieu

Oberon

Old German, meaning 'royal bear'. The Fairy King in *A Midsummer Night's Dream*.

Obie

Shortened form of Oberon, meaning 'royal bear'.

Obijulu

African, meaning 'one who has been consoled'.

Octave

(alt. Octavian, Octavio)

Latin, meaning 'eight'.

Oda

(alt. Odell, Odie, Odis)

Hebrew, meaning 'praise God'.

Ogden

Old English, meaning 'oak valley'.

Oisin

(alt. Ossian)

Celtic, meaning 'fawn'. The name of an ancient Irish poet.

Ola

Norse, meaning 'precious'.

Olaf

(alt. Olan)

Old Norse, meaning 'ancestor'.

Oleander

Hawaiian, meaning 'joyous'.

Oleg

(alt. Olen)

Russian, meaning 'holy'.

Olin

Russian, meaning 'rock'.

Oliver

Latin, meaning 'olive tree'. The UK's most popular boy's name in 2011.

Olivier

French form of Oliver, meaning 'olive tree'.

Ollie

Shortened form of Oliver, meaning 'olive tree'.

Omar

(alt. Omari, Omarion)

Arabic, meaning 'speaker'.

Ondrej

Czech, meaning 'manly'.

O

Ora
Latin, meaning 'hour'.

Oran
(alt. Oren, Orrin)
Gaelic, meaning 'light and pale'.

Orange
English, from the word 'orange'.

Orion
From the Greek hunter.

Orlando
(alt. Orlo)
Old German, meaning 'old land'. Name of a city in the USA.

Orpheus
Greek, meaning 'beautiful voice'.

Orrick
English, meaning 'sword ruler'.

Orson
Latin, meaning 'bear'.

Orville
Old French, meaning 'gold town'.

Osaka
From the Japanese city.

Osborne
Norse, meaning 'bear god'.

Oscar
Old English, meaning 'spear of the Gods'.

Osias
Hebrew, meaning 'salvation'.

Foreign alternatives
David – Dafydd, Davin
John – Jean, Giovanni, Juan
Michael – Miguel, Mikhail
Peter – Pedro, Pierre, Pyotr, Piers
Rory – Ruaridh

O

Oswald
German, meaning 'God's power'.

Otha
(alt. Otho)
German, meaning 'wealth'.

Othello
Old German, meaning 'wealth'. From the Shakespearean character.

Otis
German, meaning 'wealth'.

Otten
English, meaning 'otter-like'.

Otto
Italian, meaning 'eight'.

Ovid
Latin, meaning 'sheep'. Associated with the Roman poet.

Owain
Welsh, meaning 'youth'.

Owen
Welsh, meaning 'well born and noble'.

Oz
Hebrew, meaning 'strength'.

Palindrome names

Bob
Ebbe
Kuruk
Masam
Neven
Okko
Otto
Pip
Ramar
Uku

P

Boys' names

Pablo
Spanish, meaning 'little'.

Paco
Native American, meaning 'eagle'. Also a Spanish alternative for Francisco.

Padma
Indian, meaning 'lotus'.

Padraig
Irish, meaning 'noble'.

Panos
Greek, meaning 'all holy'.

Paolo
Italian, meaning 'little'.

Paresh
Indian, meaning 'supreme standard'.

Paris
From France's capital city. Also the Trojan prince in Homer's *Iliad* and Juliet's suitor in Shakespeare's *Romeo and Juliet*.

Pascal
Latin, meaning 'Easter child'.

Pat
Shortened form of Patrick, meaning 'noble'.

Patrice
Variant of Patrick, meaning 'noble'.

P

Patrick
Irish, meaning 'noble'.

Patten
English, meaning 'noble'.

Paul
Hebrew, meaning 'small'.

Pavel
Latin, meaning 'small'.

Pax
Latin, meaning 'peace'.

Paxton
English, meaning 'town of peace'.

Payne
Latin, meaning 'peasant'.

Payton
Latin, meaning 'peasant's town'.

Pedro
Spanish form of Peter, meaning 'rock'.

Penn
English, meaning 'hill'.

Percival
French, meaning 'pierce the valley'.

Percy
Shortened form of Percival, meaning 'pierce the valley'.

Perez
Hebrew, meaning 'breach'.

Pericles
Greek, meaning 'far-famed'.

Perrin
Greek, meaning 'rock'.

Perry
English, meaning 'rock'.

Pervis
English, meaning 'purveyor'.

Pesah
(alt. Pesach, Pesasch)
Hebrew, meaning 'spared'.

Pete
Shortened form of Peter, meaning 'rock'.

Peter

Greek, meaning 'rock'.

Petros

Greek form of Peter, meaning 'rock'.

Peyton

Old English, meaning 'fighting man's estate'.

Phil

Shortened form of Philip, meaning 'lover of horses'.

Philemon

Greek, meaning 'affectionate'.

No-nickname names

Alex
Beau
Cole
Jude
Keith
Miles
Morgan
Otto
Owen
Toby

Philip

Greek, meaning 'lover of horses'.

Philo

Greek, meaning 'love'.

Phineas

(alt. Pinchas)

Hebrew, meaning 'oracle'.

Phoenix

Greek, meaning 'dark red'.

Pierre

French form of Peter, meaning 'rock'.

Piers

Greek form of Peter, meaning 'rock'.

Pierson

Variant of Pierce, meaning 'son of Piers'.

Pip

Greek, shortened form of Philip, meaning 'lover of horses'.

P

Placido
Latin, meaning 'placid'.

Pradeep
Hindi, meaning 'light'.

Pranav
Hindi, meaning 'spiritual leader'.

Presley
Old English, meaning 'priest's meadow'.

Preston
Old English, meaning 'priest's town'.

Primo
Italian, meaning 'first'.

Primus
Latin, meaning 'first'.

Prince
English, from the word 'prince'.

Proctor
(alt. Prockter, Procter)
Latin, meaning 'steward'.

Popular South American names

Accius
Alban
Arrian
Coatl
Lucas
Matlal
Rafael
Tuco
Vincent
Zolin

Prospero
Latin, meaning 'prosperous'.

Pryor
English, meaning 'first'.

Ptolemy
Greek, meaning 'aggressive' or 'warlike'.

Purvis
(alt. Purves, Purviss)
French, meaning 'purveyor'.

 Boys' names

Qino
Chinese, meaning 'handsome'.

Quabil
Arabic, meaning 'able'.

Quadim
Arabic, meaning 'able'.

Quadir
Arabic, meaning 'powerful'.

Quaid
Irish, meaning 'fourth'.

Qued
Native American, meaning 'weaver of a decorated robe'.

Quemby
Norse, meaning 'from the woman's estate'.

Quentin
(alt. Quinten, Quintin, Quinton, Quintus)
Latin, meaning 'fifth'.

Quillan
Gaelic, meaning 'sword'.

Quillon
Gaelic, meaning 'club'.

Quincy
Old French, meaning 'estate of the fifth son'.

Quinlan

Gaelic, meaning 'fit, shapely and strong'.

Quinn

Gaelic, meaning 'counsel'.

Quinton

English, meaning 'queen's community'.

Popular North American names

Alexander
Anthony
Daniel
Ethan
Jacob
Jayden
Joshua
Michael
Noah
William

R Boys' names

Radames
Slavic, meaning 'famous joy'.

Raekwon
Hebrew, meaning 'God has healed'.

Rafael
(alt. Rafe, Rafer, Raffi, Raphael)
Hebrew, meaning 'God has healed'. One of the archangels.

Ragnar
Old Norse, meaning 'judgement warrior'.

Raheem
Arabic, meaning 'merciful and kind'.

Rahm
Hebrew, meaning 'pleasing'.

Rahul
(alt. Raoul, Raul)
Indian, meaning 'efficient'.

Raiden
(alt. Rainen)
From the Japanese god of thunder.

Rainer
Old German, meaning 'deciding warrior'.

Raj
Indian, meaning 'king'.

Rajesh
(alt. Ramesh)
Indian, meaning 'ruler of kings'.

R

Raleigh
Old English, meaning 'deer's meadow'.

Ralph
Old English, meaning 'wolf'.

Ram
English, from the word 'ram'.

Ramiro
Germanic, meaning 'powerful in battle'.

Ramone
Spanish, meaning 'wise supporter' or 'romantic'.

Ramsey
(alt. Ramsay)
Old English, meaning 'wild garlic island'.

Randall
(alt. Randolph)
Old German, meaning 'wolf shield'.

Randy
Variant of Randall, meaning 'wolf shield'. In modern English, randy can also mean amorous.

Raniel
English, meaning 'God is my happiness'.

Ranjit
Indian, meaning 'influenced by charm'.

Rannoch
Gaelic, meaning 'fern'.

Rashad
Arabic, meaning 'good judgment'.

Rasheed
(alt. Rashid)
Indian, meaning 'rightly guided'.

Rasmus
Greek, meaning 'beloved'.

Raven
English, from the word 'raven'.

Ravi
French, meaning 'delighted'.

Rawlins
French alternative of Roland, meaning 'renowned land'.

R

Ray

English, from the word 'ray'.

Raymond
(alt. Rayner)
English, meaning 'advisor'.

Raz

Israeli, meaning 'secret' or 'mystery'.

Reagan

Irish, meaning 'little king'.

Reggie

Latin, meaning 'regal'.

Reginald

Latin, meaning 'regal'.

Regis

Shortened form of Reginald, meaning 'regal'.

Reid

Old English, meaning 'by the reeds'.

Reilly

English, meaning 'courageous'.

Remington

English, meaning 'ridge town'.

Remus

Latin, meaning 'swift'.

Rémy

French, meaning 'from Rheims'.

Ren

Shortened form of Reginald, meaning 'regal'.

Renato

Latin, meaning 'rebirth'.

Rene

French, meaning 'rebirth'.

Reno

Latin, meaning 'renewed'.

Reuben

Spanish, meaning 'a son'.

Reuel

Hebrew, meaning 'friend of God'.

R

Rex

Latin, meaning 'king'.

Rey

Spanish, meaning 'king'.

Reynold

Latin, meaning 'king's advisor'.

Rhodes

German, meaning 'where the roses grow'. Also the name of the Greek town.

Rhodri

Welsh, meaning 'ruler of the circle'.

Rhys

Welsh, meaning 'enthusiasm'.

Ricardo

Spanish form of Richard, meaning 'powerful leader'.

Richard

Old German, meaning 'powerful leader'.

Richie

Shortened form of Richard,

meaning 'powerful leader'.

Rick

Shortened form of Richard, meaning 'powerful leader'.

Ricki

Shortened form of Richard, meaning 'powerful leader'.

Ricky

Shortened form of Richard, meaning 'powerful leader'.

Ridley

English, meaning 'cleared wood'.

Rigby

English, meaning 'valley of the ruler'.

Ringo

English, meaning 'ring'.

Rio

Spanish, meaning 'river'.

Riordan

Gaelic, meaning 'bard'.

R

Rishi

Variant of Richard, meaning 'powerful leader'.

Ritchie

Shortened form of Richard, meaning 'powerful leader'.

River

Latin, meaning 'river'.

Roald

Scandinavian, meaning 'ruler'.

Rob

Shortened form of Robert, meaning 'bright fame'.

Robbie

Shortened form of Robert, meaning 'bright fame'.

Robert

Old German, meaning 'bright fame'.

Roberto

Italian form of Robert, meaning 'bright fame'.

Robin

English, from the word 'robin'.

Robinson

English, meaning 'son of Robin'.

Rocco

(alt. Rocky)

Italian, meaning 'rest'.

Rockwell

English, meaning 'of the rock well'.

Rod

Short for Rhodri, Roderick and Rodney.

Roderick

German, meaning 'famous power'.

Rodney

Old German, meaning 'island near the clearing'.

Rodrigo

Spanish form of Roderick, meaning 'famous power'.

Roger

Old German, meaning 'spear man'.

R

Roland

Old German, meaning 'renowned land'.

Rolf

Old German, meaning 'wolf'.

Rollie

(alt. Rollo)

Old German, meaning 'renowned land'.

Roman

Latin, meaning 'from Rome'.

Romeo

Latin, meaning 'pilgrim to Rome'. Made famous by Shakespeare's play.

Ron

(alt. Ronnie)

Shortened form of Ronald, meaning 'mountain of strength'.

Ronald

Norse, meaning 'mountain of strength'.

Ronan

Gaelic, meaning 'little seal'.

Rory

English, meaning 'red king'.

Ross

(alt. Russ)

Scottish, meaning 'cape'.

Rowan

(alt. Roan)

Gaelic, meaning 'little red one'. Also reference to the rowan tree.

Roy

Gaelic, meaning 'red'.

Ruben

Hebrew, meaning 'son'.

Rudolph

Old German, meaning 'famous wolf'.

Rudy

Shortened form of Rudolph, meaning 'famous wolf'.

Rufus

Latin, meaning 'red-haired'.

R

Rupert

Variant of Robert, meaning 'bright fame'.

Ruslan

Russian, meaning 'like a lion'.

Russell

Old French, meaning 'little red one'.

Rusty

English, meaning 'ruddy'.

Ryan

Gaelic, meaning 'little king'.

Ryder

English, meaning 'horseman'.

Rye

English, from the word 'rye'.

Ryker

From Richard, meaning 'powerful leader'.

Rylan

English, meaning 'land where rye is grown'.

Ryley

Old English, meaning 'rye clearing'.

Ryu

Japanese, meaning 'dragon'.

R

Popular Irish names

Brian
Cian
Connor
Eoin
Finn
Kieran
Niall
Patrick
Ronan
Sean

Popular Scottish names

Alastair
Angus
Callum
Cameron
Douglas
Fraser
Hamish
Malcolm
Roderick
Stuart

S Boys' names

Saar

Hebrew, meaning 'tempest'.

Saber

French, meaning 'sword'.

Sagar

African, meaning 'ruler of the water'.

Sage

English, meaning 'wise'.

Sakari

Native American, meaning 'sweet'.

Salil

Indian, meaning 'from the water'.

Salim

Arabic, meaning 'secure'.

Salvador

Spanish, meaning 'saviour'.

Salvatore

Italian, meaning 'saviour'.

Nautical names

Caspian
Dylan
Merlin
Murphy
Neptune

S

Sam
(alt. Sama, Sammie, Sammy)
Hebrew, meaning 'God is heard'. Shortened form of Samuel.

Samir
Arabic, meaning 'pleasant companion'.

Samson
Hebrew, meaning 'son of Sam'.

Samuel
Hebrew, meaning 'God is heard'.

Sandeep
Indian, meaning 'lighting the way'.

Sandro
Shortened form of Alessandro, meaning 'defending men'.

Sandy
Shortened form of Alexander, meaning 'defending men'.

Sanjay
Indian, meaning 'victory'.

Santiago
Spanish, meaning 'Saint James'.

Santino
Spanish, meaning 'little Saint James'.

Santo
(alt. Santos)
Latin, meaning 'saint'.

Sascha
Shortened Russian form of Alexander, meaning 'defending men'.

Scott
(alt. Scottie)
English, meaning 'from Scotland'.

Seamus
Irish variant of James, meaning 'he who supplants'.

Sean
(alt. Shaun)
Variant of John, meaning 'God is gracious'.

Sebastian
Greek, meaning 'revered'.

S

Sébastien
French form of Sebastian, meaning 'revered'.

Sergio
Latin, meaning 'servant'.

Seth
Hebrew, meaning 'appointed'.

Severus
Latin, meaning 'severe'. Made popular by the character Severus Snape in the Harry Potter series.

Seymour
English, from Saint-Maur in northern France.

Shalen
Arabic, meaning 'tribal leader'.

Shane
Variant of Sean, meaning 'God is gracious'.

Sharif
Arabic, meaning 'honoured'.

Shea
Gaelic, meaning 'admirable'.

Shelby
Norse, meaning 'willow'.

Sherlock
English, meaning 'fair haired'.

Sherman
Old English, meaning 'shear man'.

Shmuel
Hebrew, meaning 'his name is God'.

Shola
Arabic, meaning 'energetic'.

Sid
Shortened form of Sidney, meaning 'wide meadow'.

Names of painters

Claude (Monet)
Francis (Bacon)
Leonardo (da Vinci)
Salvador (Dali)
Vincent (Van Gogh)

S

Sidney
English, meaning 'wide meadow'.

Sigmund
Old German, meaning 'victorious hand'.

Silvanus
(alt. Silvio)
Latin, meaning 'woods'.

Sim
Arabic, shortened form of Simba, meaning 'lion'.

Simba
Arabic, meaning 'lion'.

Simon
(alt. Simeon)
Hebrew, meaning 'to hear'.

Sinbad
Persian, meaning 'Lord of Sages'. Literary merchant adventurer.

Sindri
Norse, meaning 'dwarf'.

Sipho
African, meaning 'the unknown one'.

Sire
English, from the word 'sire'.

Sirius
Hebrew, meaning 'brightest star'. Name of Harry Potter's godfather, Sirius Black.

Skipper
English, meaning 'ship captain'.

Skyler
English, meaning 'scholar'.

Solomon
Hebrew, meaning 'peace'.

Sonny
American English, meaning 'son'.

Soren
Scandinavian, meaning 'brightest star'.

Spencer
English, meaning 'dispenser'.

S

Spike
English, from the word 'spike'.

Stamos
Greek, meaning 'reasonable'.

Stan
Shortened form of Stanley, meaning 'stony meadow'.

Stanford
English, meaning 'stone ford'.

Stanley
English, meaning 'stony meadow'.

Stavros
Greek, meaning 'crowned'.

Stellan
Latin, meaning 'starred'.

Steno
German, meaning 'stone'.

Stephen
(alt. Stefan, Stefano, Steffan)
English, meaning 'crowned'.

Steven
(alt. Steve, Stevie)
English, meaning 'crowned'.

Stewart
English, meaning 'steward'.

Stoney
English, meaning 'stone like'.

Storm
English, from the word 'storm'.

Stuart
English, meaning 'steward'.

Sven
Norse, meaning 'boy'.

Sydney
English, meaning 'wide meadow'. Also a city in Australia.

Peaceful names

Glade
Manfred
Paxton
Vale
Wilfred

Syed
Arabic, meaning 'lucky'.

Syon
Indian, meaning 'followed by good'.

Sylvester
Latin, meaning 'wooded'.

Popular Asian names

Chang
Fang
Hiro
Hiroshi
Kane
Koji
Rei
Shin
Yemon
Zinan

Popular Australian names

Cooper
Ethan
Jack
Joshua
Lachlan
Noah
Oliver
Riley
Thomas
William

T

Boys' names

Tacitus
Latin, meaning 'silent, calm'.
From the Roman historian.

Tad
English, from the word
'tadpole'.

Taine
Gaelic, meaning 'river'.

Taj
Indian, meaning 'crown'.

Takashi
Japanese, meaning
'praiseworthy'.

Takoda
Sioux, meaning 'friend to
everyone'.

Talbot
(alt. Tal)
English, an aristocratic name.

Tamir
Arabic, meaning 'tall and
wealthy'.

Taras
(alt. Tarez)
Scottish, meaning 'crag'.

Tarek
Arabic, meaning 'evening
caller'.

Tarian
Welsh, meaning 'silver'.

Tariq
Arabic, meaning 'morning star'.

179

T

Tarquin

Latin, from the Roman clan name.

Tarun

Hindi, meaning 'young'.

Tatanka

Hebrew, meaning 'bull'.

Tate

English, meaning 'cheerful'.

Taurean

English, meaning 'bull like'.

Tavares

English, meaning 'descendant of the hermit'.

Tave

(alt. Tavian, Tavis, Tavish)

French, from Gustave, meaning 'royal staff'.

Tavor

Hebrew, meaning 'misfortunate'.

Taylor

English, meaning 'tailor'.

Ted

(alt. Teddy)

English, from Edward, meaning 'wealthy guard'.

Terence

(alt. Terrill, Terry)

English, meaning 'tender'.

Tex

English, meaning 'Texan'.

Thabo

African, meaning 'filled with happiness'.

Thane

(alt. Thayer)

Scottish, meaning 'landholder'.

Thelonius

Latin, meaning 'ruler of the people'.

Theo

Shortened form of Theodore, meaning 'God's gift'.

Theodore

Greek, meaning 'God's gift'.

T

Theophile

Latin, meaning 'God's love'.

Theron

Greek, meaning 'hunter'.

Thierry

French variant of Terence, meaning 'tender'.

Thomas

Aramaic, meaning 'twin'.

Thomsen

English, meaning 'son of Thomas'.

Thor

Norse, meaning 'thunder'.

Tiago

From Santiago, meaning 'Saint James'.

Tibor

Latin, from the river Tiber.

Tien

Vietnamese, meaning 'first'.

Tieman

Gaelic, meaning 'lord'.

Tim

Shortened form of Timothy, meaning 'God's honour'.

Timothy

Greek, meaning 'God's honour'.

Tito

(alt. Titus)

Latin, meaning 'defender'.

Tobias

(alt. Toby)

Hebrew, meaning 'God is good'.

Tod

(alt. Todd)

English, meaning 'fox'.

Tom

(alt. Tomlin, Tommy)

Aramaic, meaning 'twin'.

Tonneau

French, meaning 'barrel'.

Tony

Shortened form of Anthony, from the old Roman family name.

T

Torey
Norse, meaning 'Thor'.

Torin
Gaelic, meaning 'chief'.

Torquil
Gaelic, meaning 'helmet'.

Toshi
Japanese, meaning 'reflection'.

Travis
French, meaning 'crossover'.

Trevelian
Welsh, meaning 'of the house of Eden'.

Trevor
Welsh, meaning 'great settlement'.

Trey
(alt. Tyree)
French, meaning 'very'.

Tristan
(alt. Tristram)
Celtic, from the Celtic hero.

Troy
Gaelic, meaning 'descended from the soldier'.

Tudor
Variant of Theodore, 'God's gift'.

Tyler
English, meaning 'tile maker'.

Tyrell
French, meaning 'puller'.

Tyrone
Gaelic, meaning 'Owen's county'.

Tyson
English, meaning 'son of Tyrone'.

Famous rugby players

Brian (O'Driscoll)
Gavin (Henson)
Jonny (Wilkinson)
Lawrence (Dallaglio)
Martin (Johnson)
Thom (Evans)
Toby (Flood)

Boys' names

Uberto
(alt. Umberto)
Italian, variant of Hubert, meaning 'bright or shining intellect.

Udath
(alt. Udathel)
Indian, meaning 'noble'.

Udo
German, meaning 'power of the wolf'.

Ugo
Italian form of Hugo, meaning 'mind and heart'.

Ulf
German, meaning 'wolf'.

Ulrich
German, meaning 'noble ruler'.

Ultan
Irish, meaning 'from Ulster'.

Ulysses
Greek, meaning 'wrathful'. Made famous by the mythological voyager.

Unwyn
(alt. Unwin, Unwine)
English, meaning 'unfriendly'.

Upton
English, meaning 'high town'.

Urho
Finnish, meaning 'brave'.

U

Uri
(alt. Uriah, Urias)
Hebrew, meaning 'my light'.

Uriel
Hebrew, meaning 'angel of light'. One of the archangels.

Usher
English, from the word 'usher'. Made famous by American R&B star.

Uttam
Indian, meaning 'best'.

Uzi
Hebrew, meaning 'my strength'.

Uzzi
(alt. Uzziah)
Hebrew, meaning 'my power'.

Christmas names

Christian
Ebenezer
Gabriel
Joseph
Nicholas
Noel
Wenceslas

V

Boys' names

Vaclav
Czech, meaning 'receives glory'.

Vadim
Russian, meaning 'scandal maker'.

Valdemar
German, meaning 'renowned leader'.

Valente
Latin, meaning 'valiant'.

Valentin
(alt. Val)
French, meaning 'valentine'.

Valentine
English, from the word 'valentine'.

Valentino
Italian, meaning 'valentine'.

Valerio
Italian, meaning 'valiant'.

Valia
Indian, meaning 'king of the monkeys'.

Van
Dutch, meaning 'son of'.

Vance
English, meaning 'marshland'.

V

Vangelis
Greek, meaning 'good news'.

Varun
Hindi, meaning 'water god'.

Vasilis
Greek, meaning 'kingly'.

Vaughan
Welsh, meaning 'little'.

Vernell
French, meaning 'green and flourishing'.

Verner
German, meaning 'army defender'.

Vernon
(alt. Vernie)
French, meaning 'alder grove'.

Versilius
Latin, meaning 'flier'.

Vester
Latin, meaning 'wooded'.

Vibol
Cambodian, meaning 'man of plenty'.

Victor
Latin, meaning 'champion'.

Vidal
(alt. Vidar)
Spanish, meaning 'life giving'.

Vijay
Hindi, meaning 'conquering'.

Vikram
Hindi, meaning 'sun'.

Viktor
Latin, meaning 'victory'.

Ville
French, meaning 'town'.

Vincent
(alt. Vince)
English, meaning 'victorious'.

Virgil
Latin, meaning 'staff bearer'. From the Latin poet.

Vito
Spanish, meaning 'life'.

Vittorio
Italian, meaning 'victory'.

Vitus

Latin, meaning 'life'.

Vivek

Indian, meaning 'wisdom'.

Vivian

Latin, meaning 'lively'.

Vladimir

Slavic, meaning 'prince'.

Volker

German, meaning 'defender of the people'.

Von

Norse, meaning 'hope'.

V

Shakespearean names

Angelo *(Measure for Measure)*
Anthony *(Anthony and Cleopatra)*
Balthazar *(Romeo and Juliet)*
Hamlet *(Hamlet)*
Henry *(Henry V)*
Iago *(Othello)*
Othello *(Othello)*
Richard *(Richard III)*
Romeo *(Romeo and Juliet)*
Sebastian *(Twelfth Night)*

W

Boys' names

Wade

English, meaning 'to move forward' or 'to go'.

Waldemar

German, meaning 'famous ruler'.

Walden

English, meaning 'valley of the Britons'.

Waldo

Old German, meaning 'rule'.

Walker

English, meaning 'a fuller'.

Wallace

English, meaning 'foreigner' or 'stranger'.

Wally

German, meaning 'ruler of the army'.

Walter

(alt. Walt)

German, meaning 'ruler of the army'.

Wasim

Arabic, meaning 'attractive' or 'full of grace'.

Ward

English, meaning 'guardian'.

Wardell

Old English, meaning 'watchman's hill'.

Warner
German, meaning 'army guard'.

Warren
German, meaning 'guard' or 'the game park'.

Warwick
English, meaning 'farm near the weir'.

Washington
English, meaning 'clever' or 'clever man's settlement'.

Wassily
Greek, meaning 'royal' or 'kingly'.

Watson
English, meaning 'son' or 'son of Walter'.

Waverley
(alt. Waverly)
English, meaning 'quaking aspen'.

Waylon
English, meaning 'land by the road'.

Wayne
English, meaning 'a cartwright'.

Webster
English, meaning 'weaver'.

Weldon
English, meaning 'from the hill of well' or 'hill with a well'.

Wendell
(alt. Wendel)
German, meaning 'a wend'.

Werner
German, meaning 'army guard'.

Werther
German, meaning 'a soldier in the army'.

Weston
English, meaning 'from the west town'.

Wheeler
English, meaning 'wheel maker'.

Whitley
English, meaning 'white wood'.

Whitman

Old English, meaning 'white man'.

Whitney

Old English, meaning 'white island'.

Wilber
(alt. Wilbur)

Old German, meaning 'bright will'.

Wildon

English, meaning 'wooded hill'.

Wiley

Old English, meaning 'beguiling' or 'enchanting'.

Wilford

Old English, meaning 'the ford by the willows'.

Wilfredo
(alt. Wilfred, Wilfrid)

English, meaning 'to will peace'.

Wilhelm

German, meaning 'strong-willed warrior'.

Wilkes
(alt. Wilkie)

Old English, meaning 'strong-willed protector' or 'strong and resolute protector'.

William
(alt. Will, Willie)

English (Teutonic), meaning 'strong protector' or 'strong-willed warrior'.

Willis

English, meaning 'server of William'.

Willoughby

Old Norse and Old English, meaning 'from the farm by the trees'.

Wilmer

English (Teutonic), meaning 'famously resolute'.

Wilmot

English, meaning 'resolute mind'.

Wilson

English, meaning 'son of William'.

W

Wilton

Old Norse and English, meaning 'from the farm by the brook' or 'from the farm by the streams'.

Windell

(alt. Wendell)

German, meaning 'wanderer' or 'seeker'.

> ### Knights of the round table
>
> Arthur
> Gareth
> Gawain
> Lancelot
> Tristram
>
>

Windsor

Old English, meaning 'river bank' or 'landing place'.

Winfield

English, meaning 'from the field of Wina'.

Winslow

Old English, meaning 'victory on the hill'.

Winter

Old English, meaning 'to be born in the winter'.

Winthrop

Old English, meaning 'village of friends'.

Winton

Old English, meaning 'a friend's farm'.

Wirrin

Aboriginal, meaning 'a tea tree'.

Wistan

Old English, meaning 'battle stone' or 'mark of the battle'.

Wittan

Old English, meaning 'farm in the woods' or 'farm by the woods'.

Wolf

(alt. Wolfe)

English, meaning 'strong as a wolf'.

Wolfgang

Teutonic, meaning 'the path of wolves'.

Wolfrom

Teutonic, meaning 'raven wolf'.

Wolter

Dutch, a form of Walter meaning 'ruler of the army'.

Woodburn

Old English, meaning 'a stream in the woods'.

Woodrow

English, meaning 'from the row of houses by the wood'.

Woodward

English, meaning 'guardian of the forest'.

Woody

American, meaning 'path in the woods'.

Worcester

Old English, meaning 'from a Roman site'.

Worth

American, meaning 'worth much' or 'wealthy place' or 'wealth and riches'.

Wren

Old English, meaning 'tiny bird'.

Wright

Old English, meaning 'to be a craftsman' or 'from a carpenter'.

Wyatt

Teutonic, meaning 'from wood' or 'from the wide water'.

Wyclef
(alt. Wycleff, Wycliff, Wycliffe)

English, meaning 'inhabitant of the white cliff'.

Wynn
(alt. Wyn)

Welsh, meaning 'very blessed' or 'the fair blessed one'.

Popular Welsh names

Aeron	Gareth
Aled	Gwyn
Bryn	Owain
Dylan	Rhys
Evan	Wallace

X Boys' names

Xadrian

American, a combination of X and Adrian, meaning 'from Hadria'.

Xander

Greek, meaning 'defender of the people'.

Xannon

American, meaning 'descendent of an ancient family'.

Xanthus

Greek, meaning 'golden-haired'.

Xavier

Latin, meaning 'to the new house'.

Xenon

Greek, meaning 'the guest'.

Xerxes

Persian, meaning 'ruler of the people' or 'respected king'.

Xeven

Slavic, meaning 'lively'.

Xylander

Greek, meaning 'man of the forest'.

Bird names

Gannet
Phoenix
Robin
Tern
Wren

195

Long names

Alexander
Bartholomew
Christopher
Demetrius
Giovanni
Montgomery
Obadiah
Roberto
Salvatore
Zachariah

Popular Spanish names

Alejandro
Carlos
Diego
Ivan
Javier
Jorge
Marcos
Mario
Pablo
Raul

Y

Boys' names

Yaal

Hebrew, meaning 'ascending' or 'one to ascend'.

Yadid

Hebrew, meaning 'the beloved one'.

Yadon

Hebrew, meaning 'against judgment'.

Yahir

Spanish, meaning 'handsome one'.

Yaholo

Native American, meaning 'yells'.

Yakiya

Hebrew, meaning 'pure' or 'bright'.

Yair

Hebrew, meaning 'the enlightening one' or 'illuminating'.

Yanis
(alt. Yannis)

Greek, a form of John meaning 'gift of God'.

Yarden

Hebrew, meaning 'to flow downward'.

Ye

Chinese, meaning 'bright one' or 'light'.

Yehuda

Hebrew, meaning 'to praise and exalt'.

Yered

Hebrew, a form of Jared, meaning 'descending'.

Yerik

Russian, meaning 'God-appointed one'.

Yerodin

African, meaning 'studious'.

Yervant

Armenian, meaning 'King of people'.

Yitzak
(alt. Yitzaak)

Hebrew, meaning 'laughter' or 'one who laughs'.

Ynyr

Welsh, meaning 'to honour'.

Yobachi

African, meaning 'one who prays to God' or 'prayed to God'.

Yogi

Japanese, meaning 'one who practises yoga' or 'from yoga'.

Yoloti

Aztec, meaning 'heart'.

Yona

Native American, meaning 'bear'; and also Hebrew, meaning 'dove'.

York

Celtic, meaning 'yew tree' or 'from the farm of the yew tree'.

Yosef

Hebrew, meaning 'added by God' or 'God shall add'.

Yuri

Aboriginal, meaning 'to hear'; Japanese, meaning 'one to listen'; Russian, a form of George meaning 'farmer'.

Yuuta

Japanese, meaning 'excellent'.

Yves

French, meaning 'miniature archer' or 'small archer'.

Z Boys' names

Zachariah
(alt. Zac, Zach, Zachary)
Hebrew, meaning 'remembered by the Lord' or 'God has remembered'.

Zad
Persian, meaning 'my son'.

Zada
(alt. Zadan, Zadin, Zadun)
Dutch, meaning 'a man who sowed seeds'.

Zadok
Hebrew, meaning 'righteous one'.

Zador
Hungarian, meaning 'violent demeanour'.

Zafar
Arabic, meaning 'triumphant'.

Zaid
African, meaning 'increase the growth' or 'growth'.

Zaide
Yiddish, meaning 'the elder ones'.

Zain
(alt. Zane)
Arabic, meaning 'the handsome son'.

Zaire
African, meaning 'river from Zaire'.

Zander

Greek, meaning 'defender of my people'.

Zarek

Persian, meaning 'God protect our King'.

Zoltan

(alt. Zoltin)

Hungarian, meaning 'life'.

Fiery names

Aidan

Blaze

Flint

Kenneth

part three

Girls' Names

A Girls' names

A'mari

Variation of the Swahili or Muslim name Amira, meaning 'princess'.

Aanya

Variation of the Russian name Anya, meaning 'favour' or 'grace'. Also Sanskrit, meaning 'the inexhaustible'.

Aaryanna

Derivative of the Latin and Greek name Ariadne, both meaning 'the very holy one'.

Abby
(alt. Abbey, Abbie)

Form of Abigail, Hebrew, meaning 'my father's joy'.

Abigail
(alt. Abagail, Abbiegayle, Abbigail, Abigale, Abigayle)

Hebrew, meaning 'my father's joy'.

Abilene
(alt. Abilee)

Latin and Spanish for 'hazelnut'.

Abina
(alt. Abena)

Ghanaian, meaning 'born on Tuesday'.

Abra

Female variation of Abraham. Also Sanskrit, meaning 'clouds'.

A

Abril

Spanish for the month of April. Also Latin, meaning 'open'.

Acacia

Greek, meaning 'point' or 'thorn'. Also a species of flowering trees and shrubs.

Acadia

Variation of the Greek word arcadia meaning 'paradise'. Originally, a French colony in Canada.

Ada

(alt. Adair)

Hebrew, meaning 'adornment'.

Adalee

German, meaning 'noble'.

Adalia

Hebrew, meaning 'God is my refuge'.

Addie

(alt. Addy, Adi)

Shortened form of Addison, Adelaide, Adele and Adeline.

Addison

(alt. Addisyn, Addyson)

English, meaning 'son of Adam'.

Adelaide

(alt. Adelaida)

German, popular after the rule of William IV and Queen Adelaide of England in the 19th century.

Adele

(alt. Adela, Adelia, Adell, Adella, Adelle)

German, meaning 'noble' or 'nobility'.

Adeline

(alt. Adalyn, Adalynn, Adelina, Adelyn)

Variant of Adelaide, meaning 'noble'.

Aden

(alt. Addien)

Hebrew, meaning 'decoration'.

Aderyn

Welsh, meaning 'bird'.

Adesina

Nigerian, meaning 'she paves the way'. Usually given to a firstborn daughter.

A

Adeola
(alt. Adeolah, Adeolla)

African, meaning 'weaver of a crown of honour'.

Adia

Variant of Ada, meaning 'adornment'.

Adina
(alt. Adena)

Hebrew, meaning 'high hopes' or 'precious'.

Adira

Hebrew, meaning 'noble' or 'powerful'.

Adrian

Italian, from the northern city of Hadria.

Adrianna
(alt. Adriana)

Variant of Adrienne, meaning 'rich' or 'dark'.

Adrienne
(alt. Adriane, Adrianne)

Greek, meaning 'rich', or Latin, meaning 'dark'.

Aegle

Greek, meaning 'brightness' or 'splendour'.

Movie inspirations

Bridget (*Bridget Jones's Diary*)
Cady (*Mean Girls*)
Fiona (*Shrek*)
Holly (*Breakfast at Tiffany's*)
Isabella, Bella (*Twilight*)
Lara (*Tomb Raider*)
Maria (*The Sound of Music*)
Marla (*Fight Club*)
Mary (*Mary Poppins*)
Nina (*Black Swan*)
Pandora (*Avatar*)
Trinity (*The Matrix*)

A

Aerin

Variant of Erin, meaning 'peace-making'.

Aerith

American, from a character in the computer game *Final Fantasy VII*.

Aero
(alt. Aeron)

Greek, meaning 'water'.

Aerolynn

Combination of the Greek Aero, meaning 'water', and the English Lynn, meaning 'waterfall'.

Afia
(alt. Aff, Affi)

Arabic, meaning 'a child born on Friday'.

Africa

Celtic, meaning 'pleasant', as well as the name of the continent.

Afsaneh

Iranian, meaning 'a fairy tale'.

Afsha

Persian, meaning 'one who sprinkles light'.

Afton

Originally a place name in Scotland.

Agatha

From Saint Agatha, the patron saint of bells, meaning 'good'.

Aglaia

One of the three Greek Graces, meaning 'brilliance'.

Agnes

Greek, meaning 'virginal' or 'pure'.

Agrippina

Latin, from the expression, meaning 'born feet first'.

Aida

Arabic, meaning 'reward' or 'present'.

Aidanne
(alt. Aidan, Aidenn)

Gaelic, meaning 'fire'.

Ailbhe

Irish, meaning 'noble' or 'bright'.

A

Aileen
(alt. Aelinn, Aleen, Aline, Alline, Eileen)
Gaelic variant of Helen, meaning 'light'.

Ailith
(alt. Ailish)
Old English, meaning 'seasoned warrior'.

Ailsa
Scottish, meaning 'pledge from God', as well as the name of a Scottish island, Ailsa Craig.

Aimee
(alt. Aimie, Amie)
French form of Amy, meaning 'beloved'.

Aina
Scandinavian, meaning 'forever'.

Aine
(alt. Aino)
Celtic, meaning 'happiness'.

Ainsley
Scottish and Gaelic, meaning 'one's own meadow'.

Aisha
(alt. Aeysha)
Arabic, meaning 'woman'; as well as Swahili, meaning 'life'.

Aishwarya
Variant of the Arabic Aisha, meaning 'woman'.

Aislinn
(alt. Aislin, Aisling, Aislyn, Alene, Allene)
Irish Gaelic, meaning 'dream'.

Aiyanna
(alt. Aiyana)
Native American, meaning 'forever flowering'.

Aja
Hindi, meaning 'goat'.

Aka
(alt. Akah, Akkah)
Maori, meaning 'loving one'.

Akela
(alt. Akilah)
Hawaiian, meaning 'noble'.

Akilina
Greek or Russian, meaning 'eagle'.

Akiva

Hebrew, meaning 'protect and shelter'.

Alaina

(alt. Alane, Alani, Alayna, Aleena)

Feminine of Alan, from the Gaelic for 'rock' or 'comely'.

Alana

(alt. Alanna, Alannah)

Variant of Alaina, meaning 'rock' or 'comely'.

Alanis

(alt. Alarice)

Variant of Alaina, meaning 'rock' or 'comely'.

Alba

Latin, meaning 'white'. Also the Gaelic word for 'Scotland'.

Alberta

(alt. Albertha, Albertine)

Feminine of Albert, from the Old German for 'noble, bright, famous'.

Albina

Latin, meaning 'white' or 'fair'.

Alda

German, meaning 'old' or 'prosperous'.

Aldis

English, meaning 'battle-seasoned'.

Aleah

Arabic, meaning 'high', or Persian, meaning 'one of God's beings'.

Aleta

(alt. Aletha)

Greek, meaning 'footloose'.

Alethea

(alt. Aletheia)

Greek, meaning 'truth'.

Alex

(alt. Alexa, Alexi, Alexia, Alexina)

Shortened version of Alexandra, meaning 'man's defender'.

Alexandra

(alt. Alejandra, Alejhandra, Aleksandra, Alessandra, Alexandria)

Feminine of Alexander, from the Greek interpretation of 'man's defender'.

A

Alexis

(alt. Alexus, Alexys)

Greek, meaning 'helper'.

Aleydis

Variant of Alice, meaning 'noble' or 'nobility'.

Alfreda

Old English, meaning 'elf power'.

Ali

(alt. Allie, Ally)

Shortened version of Alexandra, Aliyah or Alice.

Alibeth

Variant of Elizabeth, meaning 'consecrated to God'.

Alice

(alt. Alize, Alyce, Alys, Alyse)

English, meaning 'noble' or 'nobility'.

Alicia

(alt. Ahlicia, Alecia, Alesia, Alessia, Alizia, Alycia, Alysia)

Variant of Alice, meaning 'nobility'.

Alida

(alt. Aleida)

Latin, meaning 'small winged one'.

Alienor

(alt. Aliana)

Variant of Eleanor, from the Greek for 'light'.

Aliki

(alt. Alika)

Variant of Alice, meaning 'nobility'.

Alima

Arabic, meaning 'cultured'.

Alina

(alt. Alena)

Slavic variation of Helen, meaning 'light'.

Alisha

(alt. Alesha, Alysha)

Variant of Alice, meaning 'nobility'.

Alison

(alt. Allison, Allisyn, Allyson, Alyson)

Variant of Alice, meaning 'nobility'.

Alissa
(alt. Alessa, Alise)

Greek, meaning 'pretty'.

Alivia
Variant of Olivia, meaning 'olive tree'.

Aliya
(alt. Aaliyah, Aleah, Alia, Aliah, Aliyah)

Arabic, meaning 'exalted' or 'sublime'.

Alla
Variant of Ella or Alexandra. Also a possible reference to Allah.

Allegra
Italian, meaning 'joyous'.

Allura
French, from the word for entice, meaning 'the power of attraction'.

Allyn
Feminine of Alan, meaning 'peaceful'.

Alma
Three possible origins: Latin for 'giving nurture', Italian for 'soul' and Arabic for 'learned'.

Almeda
(alt. Almeta)

Latin, meaning 'ambitious'.

Almera
(alt. Almira)

Feminine of Elmer, from the Arabic for 'aristocratic' and the Old English meaning 'noble'.

Alohi
Variant of the Hawaiian greeting Aloha, meaning 'love and affection'.

Alona
Hebrew, meaning 'oak tree'.

Alora
Variant of Alona, meaning 'oak tree'.

Alpha
The first letter of the Greek alphabet, usually given to a firstborn daughter.

Alta
Latin, meaning 'elevated'.

Altagracia

Spanish, meaning 'grace'.

Althea

(alt. Altea, Altha)

Greek, meaning 'healing power'.

Alva

Spanish, meaning 'blonde' or 'fair skinned'.

Alvena

(alt. Alvina)

English, meaning 'noble friend'.

Alvia

(alt. Alyvia)

Variant of Olivia, meaning 'olive tree' or Elvira from the ancient Spanish city.

Alyssa

(alt. Alisa Allyssa, Alysa)

Greek, meaning 'rational'.

Amabel

Variant of Annabel, meaning 'grace and beauty'.

Amadea

Feminine of Amadeus, meaning 'God's'.

Amalia

Variant of Emilia, Latin, meaning 'rival, eager'.

Amana

Hebrew, meaning 'loyal and true'.

Amanda

Latin, meaning 'much loved'.

Amandine

Variant of Amanda, meaning 'much loved'.

Amara

(alt. Amani)

Greek, meaning 'lovely forever'.

Amarantha

Contraction of Amanda and Samantha, meaning 'much loved listener'.

Amaris

(alt. Amari, Amasa, Amata, Amaya)

Hebrew, meaning 'pledged by God'.

Amaryllis

Greek, meaning 'fresh'. Also a flower by the same name.

Amber

French, from the word for the semi-precious stone of the same name.

Amberly

Contraction of Amber and Leigh, meaning 'stone' and 'meadow'.

Amberlynn

Contraction of Amber and Lynn, meaning 'stone' and 'waterfall'.

Amboree
(alt. Amber, Ambree)

American, meaning 'precocious'.

Amelia
(alt. Aemilia)

Greek, meaning 'industrious'.

Amelie
(alt. Amalie)

French form of Amelia, meaning 'industrious'.

America

From the country of the same name.

Ameris

Variant of Amaryllis, meaning 'fresh'.

Amethyst

Greek, from the word for the precious, mulberry coloured stone of the same name.

Amina

Arabic, meaning 'honest and trustworthy'.

Amira
(alt. Amiya, Amiyah)

Arabic, meaning 'a high-born girl'.

Amity

Latin, meaning 'friendship and harmony'.

Amory

Variant of the Spanish name Amor, meaning 'love'.

Amy
(alt. Amee, Ami, Amie, Ammie)

Latin, meaning 'beloved'.

Amya

Variant of Amy, meaning 'beloved'.

Ana-Lisa

Contraction of Anna and Lisa, meaning 'grace' or 'consecrated to God'.

Anafa

Hebrew, meaning 'heron'.

Ananda

Hindi, meaning 'bliss'.

Anastasia

(alt. Athanasia)

Greek, meaning 'resurrection'.

Anatolia

From the eastern Greek town of the same name.

Andelyn

Contraction of the feminine for Andrew and Lynn, meaning 'strong waterfall'.

Andrea

(alt. Andreia, Andria)

Feminine of Andrew, from the Greek term for 'a man's woman'.

Andrine

Variant of Andrea, meaning 'a man's woman'.

Andromeda

Greek, meaning 'leader of men'. From the heroine of a Greek legend.

Anemone

Greek, meaning 'breath'. Also from the flower.

Angela

(alt. Angel, Angeles, Angelia Angelle, Angie)

Greek, meaning 'messenger from God' or 'angel'.

Angelica

(alt. Angelina, Angeline, Angelique, Angelise, Angelita, Anjelica)

Latin, meaning 'angelic'.

Anise

(alt. Anisa, Anissa)

French, from the licorice flavoured plant of the same name.

Anita

(alt. Anitra)

Variant of Ann, meaning 'grace'.

Ann

(alt. Anne, Annie)

Derived from Hannah, meaning 'grace'.

213

Anna
(alt. Ana, Anne)
Derived from Hannah, meaning 'grace'.

Annabel
(alt. Anabel, Anabelle, Annabell, Annabella, Annabelle)
Contraction of Anna and Belle, meaning 'grace' and 'beauty'.

Annalise
(alt. Annalee, Annaliese, Annalisa, Anneli, Annelie, Annelies, Annelise)
Contraction of Anna and Lise, meaning 'grace' and 'pledged to God'.

Annemarie
(alt. Annamae, Annamarie, Annelle, Annmarie)
Contraction of Anna and Mary, meaning 'grace' and 'star of the sea'.

Annette
(alt. Annetta)
Derived from Hannah, Hebrew, meaning 'grace'.

Annis
Greek, meaning 'finished or completed'.

Annora
Latin, meaning 'honour'.

Anoushka
(alt. Anousha)
Russian variant of Ann, meaning 'grace'.

Ansley
English, meaning 'the awesome one's meadow'.

Anthea
(alt. Anthi)
Greek, meaning 'flowerlike'.

Antigone
In Greek mythology, Antigone was the daughter of Oedipus.

Antoinette
(alt. Anonetta, Antonette, Antonietta)
Both a variation of Ann and the feminine of Anthony, meaning 'invaluable grace'.

Antonia
(alt. Antonella, Antonina)
Latin, meaning 'invaluable'.

Anwen
Welsh, meaning 'very fair'.

Anya
(alt. Aniya, Aniyah, Aniylah, Anja)

Russian, meaning 'grace'.

Apollonia
Feminine of Apollo, the Greek god of the sun.

Apple
From the name of the fruit.

April
(alt. Avril)

Latin, meaning 'opening up'. Also the name of the month.

Aquilina
(alt. Aqua, Aquila)

Spanish, meaning 'like an eagle'.

Ara
Arabic, meaning 'brings rain'.

Arabella
Latin, meaning 'answered prayer'.

Araceli
(alt. Aracely)

Spanish, meaning 'altar of Heaven'.

Araylia
(alt. Araelea)

Latin, meaning 'golden'.

Arcadia
Greek, meaning 'paradise'.

Ardelle
(alt. Ardell, Ardella)

Latin, meaning 'burning with enthusiasm'.

Arden
(alt. Ardis, Ardith)

Latin, meaning 'burning with enthusiasm'.

Arella
(alt. Areli, Arely)

Hebrew, meaning 'angel'.

Aretha
Greek, meaning 'woman of virtue'.

Aria
(alt. Ariah)

Italian, meaning 'melody'.

A

Ariadne

Greek and Latin, meaning 'the very holy one'. In Greek mythology, Ariadne was the daughter of King Minos.

Ariana

(alt. Ariane, Arianna, Arienne)

Welsh, meaning 'silver'.

Ariel

(alt. Ariela, Ariella, Arielle)

Hebrew, meaning 'lioness of God'. One of the archangels.

Arlene

(alt. Arleen, Arlie, Arline, Arly)

Gaelic, meaning 'pledge'.

Armida

Latin, meaning 'little armed one'.

Artemisia

(alt. Artemis)

Greek and Spanish, meaning 'perfect'.

Artie

(alt. Arti)

Shortened form of Artemisia, meaning 'perfect'.

Ashanti

From the geographical area in Ghana, Africa.

Ashby

English, meaning 'ash tree farm'. Also name of place in Leicestershire.

Ashley

(alt. Ashely, Ashlee, Ashleigh, Ashli, Ashlie, Ashly)

English, meaning 'ash tree meadow'.

Ashlynn

(alt. Ashlyn)

Irish Gaelic, meaning 'dream'.

Ashton

(alt. Ashtyn)

Old English, meaning 'ash tree town'. From the place name.

Asia

From the name of the continent.

Asma

(alt. Asmara)

Arabic, meaning 'high-standing'.

Aspen
(alt. Aspynn)

From the name of the tree. Also name of a city in the USA.

Assumpta
(alt. Assunta)

Italian, meaning 'raised up'.

Asta
(alt. Asteria, Astor, Astoria)

Greek or Latin, meaning 'star-like'.

Astrid

Old Norse, meaning 'beautiful like a God'.

Atara

Hebrew, meaning 'diadem'.

Athena
(alt. Athenais)

Greek, meaning 'wise'. From the Greek goddess of wisdom.

Aubrey
(alt. Aubree, Aubriana, Aubrie)

French, meaning 'elf ruler'.

Audrey
(alt. Audra, Audrie, Audrina, Audry, Autry)

English, meaning 'noble strength'.

Audrina

Variant of Audrey, meaning 'noble strength'.

Augusta
(alt. August, Augustine)

Latin, meaning 'worthy of respect'.

Aura
(alt. Aurea)

Greek or Latin, meaning either 'soft breeze' or 'gold'.

Aurelia
(alt. Aurelie)

Latin, meaning 'gold'.

Aurora
(alt. Aurore)

Latin, meaning 'dawn'. In Roman mythology, Aurora was the goddess of sunrise.

Austine
(alt. Austen, Austin)
Latin, meaning 'worthy of respect'.

Autumn
From the name of the season

Ava
(alt. Avia, Avie)
Latin, meaning 'like a bird'.

Avalon
(alt. Avalyn, Aveline)
Celtic, meaning 'island of apples'.

Axelle
Greek, meaning 'father of peace'.

Aya
(alt. Ayah)
Hebrew, meaning 'bird'.

Ayanna
(alt. Ayana)
American, meaning 'grace'.

Ayesha
(alt. Aisha, Aysha)
Persian, meaning 'small one'.

Azalea
Latin, meaning 'dry earth'.

Azalia
Hebrew, meaning 'aided by God'.

Aziza
Hebrew, meaning 'mighty', or Arabic, meaning 'precious'.

Azure
(alt. Azaria)
French, meaning 'sky-blue'.

Popular French names

Adele	Giselle
Amelie	Monique
Belle	Paulette
Colette	Sabine
Fleur	Yvette

A

 Girls' names

Babette

French version of Barbara, from the Greek word meaning 'foreign'.

Badia

(alt. Badiyn, Badea)

Arabic, meaning 'elegant'.

Bailey

(alt. Baeli, Bailee)

English, meaning 'law enforcer'.

Bambi

Shortened version of the Italian Bambina, meaning 'child'.

Barbara

(alt. Barb, Barbie, Barbra)

Greek, meaning 'foreign'.

Basma

Arabic, meaning 'smile'.

Bathsheba

Hebrew, meaning 'daughter of the oath'.

Bay

(alt. Baya)

From the plant or geographical name.

Beata

Latin, meaning 'blessed'.

Beatrice

(alt. Beatrix, Beatriz, Bellatrix, Betrys)

Latin, meaning 'bringer of gladness'.

B

Literary names

Alice (*Alice in Wonderland*, Lewis Carroll)
Bella (Twilight novels, Stephanie Meyer)
Charlotte (*The Sorrows of Young Werther*, J. W. von Goethe)
Emma (*Madame Bovary*, Gustave Flaubert)
Esther (*Bleak House*, Charles Dickens)
Iris (*The Blind Assassin*, Margaret Atwood)
Hermione (Harry Potter series, J K Rowling)
Lyra (*His Dark Materials*, Phillip Pullman)
Matilda (*Matilda*, Roald Dahl)
Shirley (*Shirley*, Charlotte Brontë)
Wendy (*Peter Pan*, J M Barrie)

Becky
(alt. Beccie, Beccy, Beckie)

Shortened form of Rebecca, Hebrew meaning 'joined'.

Bee

Shortened form of Beatrice, meaning 'bringer of gladness'.

Belinda
(alt. Belen, Belina)

Contraction of Belle and Linda, meaning 'beautiful'.

Bell

Shortened form of Isabel, meaning 'pledged to God'.

Bella

Latin, meaning 'beautiful'.

Belle

French, meaning 'beautiful'.

Belva

Latin, meaning 'beautiful view'.

Bénédicta

Latin, the feminine of Benedict, meaning 'blessed'.

Benita
(alt. Bernita)

Spanish, meaning 'blessed'.

Bennie

Shortened version of Bénédicta and Benita, meaning 'blessed'.

Berit

(alt. Beret)

Scandinavian, meaning 'splendid' or 'gorgeous'.

Bernadette

French, meaning 'courageous'.

Bernadine

French, meaning 'courageous'.

Bernice

(alt. Berenice, Berniece, Burnice)

Greek, meaning 'she who brings victory'.

Bertha

(alt. Berta, Berthe, Bertie)

German, meaning 'bright'.

Beryl

Greek, meaning 'pale green gemstone'.

Bess

(alt. Bessie)

Shortened form of Elizabeth, meaning 'consecrated to God'.

Beth

Hebrew, meaning 'house'. Also shortened form of Elizabeth, meaning 'consecrated to God'.

Bethany

(alt. Bethan)

Hebrew, referring to a geographical location.

Bethel

Hebrew, meaning 'house of God'.

Bettina

Spanish version of Elizabeth, meaning 'consecrated to God'.

Betty

(alt. Betsy, Bette, Bettie, Bettye)

Shortened version of Elizabeth, meaning 'consecrated to God'.

Beulah

Hebrew, meaning 'married'.

Beverly

(alt. Beverlee, Beverley)

English, meaning 'beaver stream'.

Bevin

Celtic, meaning 'fair lady'.

Beyoncé

American, made popular by the singer.

Bianca

(alt. Blanca)

Italian, meaning 'white'.

Bibiana

Greek, meaning 'alive'.

Bijou

French, meaning 'jewel'.

Billie

(alt. Bill, Billy, Billye)

Shortened version of Wilhelmina, meaning 'determined'.

Bina

Hebrew, meaning 'knowledge'.

Birgit

(alt. Birgitta)

Norwegian, meaning 'splendid'.

Blair

Scottish Gaelic, meaning 'flat, plain area'.

Blake

(alt. Blakely, Blakelyn)

English, meaning either 'pale-skinned' or 'dark'.

Blanche

(alt. Blanch)

French, meaning 'white or pale'.

Bliss

English, meaning 'intense happiness'.

Blithe

English, meaning 'joyous'.

Blodwen

Welsh, meaning 'white flower'.

Blossom

English, meaning 'flowerlike'.

Blythe

(alt. Bly)

English, meaning 'happy and carefree'.

Bobbi

(alt. Bobbie, Bobby)

Shortened version of Roberta, meaning 'bright fame'.

B

Bonamy
(alt. Bomani, Bonamia, Bonamea)

French, meaning 'close friend'.

Bonita
Spanish, meaning 'pretty'.

Bonnie
(alt. Bonny)

Scottish, meaning 'fair of face'.

Brandy
(alt. Brandee, Brandi, Brandie)

From the name of the liquor.

Branwen
Welsh, meaning 'a white crow'.

Brea
(alt. Bree, Bria)

Shortened form of Brianna, meaning 'strong'.

Brenda
Old Norse, meaning 'sword'.

Brianna
(alt. Breana, Breanna, Breanne)

Irish Gaelic, meaning 'strong'.

Bridget
(alt. Bridgett, Bridgette, Brigette, Brigid, Brigitta, Brigitte)

Irish Gaelic, meaning 'strength and power'.

Brier
French, meaning 'heather'.

Biblical names

Abigail
Delilah
Eve
Hannah
Mary
Naomi
Rebecca
Ruth
Sarah
Salome

B

Brit
(alt. Britt, Britta)

Celtic, meaning 'spotted' or 'freckled'.

Britannia

Latin, meaning 'Britain'.

Brittany
(alt. Britany, Britney, Britni, Brittani, Brittanie, Brittney, Brittni, Brittny)

Latin, meaning 'from England'.

Bronwyn
(alt. Bronwen)

Welsh, meaning 'fair breast'.

Brooke
(alt. Brook)

English, meaning 'small stream'.

Brooklyn
(alt. Brooklynn)

From the name of a New York borough.

Brunhilda

German, meaning 'armour-wearing fighting maid'.

Bryn
(alt. Brynn)

Welsh, meaning 'mount'.

Bryony
(alt. Briony)

From the name of a European vine.

Buffy

American alternative of Elizabeth, meaning 'consecrated to God'.

Popular Spanish names

Ana
Carla
Carmen
Daniela
Elena
Marina
Maria
Natalia
Sara
Sofia

B

 Girls' names

Cadew
French, meaning 'gift'.

Cadence
Latin, meaning 'with rhythm'.

Cai
Vietnamese, meaning 'feminine'.

Caitlin
(alt. Cadyn, Caitlann, Caitlyn, Caitlynn)
Greek, meaning 'pure'.

Calandra
Greek, meaning 'lark'.

Calantha
(alt. Calanthe)
Greek, meaning 'lovely flower'.

Caledonia
Latin, meaning 'from Scotland'.

Calia
American, meaning 'renowned beauty'.

Calla
Greek, meaning 'beautiful'.

Callie
(alt. Caleigh, Cali, Calleigh, Cally)
Greek, meaning 'beauty'.

Calliope
Greek, meaning 'beautiful voice'. From the muse of epic poetry in Greek mythology.

Callista
(alt. Callisto)
Greek, meaning 'most beautiful'.

Camas

Native American, from the root and bulb of the same name.

Cambria

Welsh, from the alternative name for Wales.

Camden
(alt. Camdyn)

English, meaning 'winding valley'.

Cameo

Italian, meaning 'skin'.

Cameron
(alt. Camryn)

Scottish Gaelic, meaning 'bent nose'.

Camilla
(alt. Camelia, Camellia, Camila, Camillia)

Latin, meaning 'spiritual serving girl'.

Camille

Latin, meaning 'spiritual serving girl'.

Candace
(alt. Candice, Candis)

Latin, meaning 'brilliant white'.

Candida

Latin, meaning 'white'.

Candra

Latin, meaning 'glowing'.

Candy
(alt. Candi)

Shortened form of Candace, meaning 'brilliant white'.

Canei

Greek, meaning 'pure'.

Caoimhe

Celtic, meaning 'gentleness'.

Caprice

Italian, meaning 'ruled by whim'.

Cara

Latin, meaning 'darling'.

Caren
(alt. Carin, Caron, Caryn)

Greek, meaning 'pure'.

Carey

(alt. Cari, Carie, Carri, Carrie, Cary)

Welsh, meaning 'near the castle'.

Carina

(alt. Corina)

Italian, meaning 'dearest little one'.

Carissa

(alt. Carisa)

Greek, meaning 'grace'.

Carla

(alt. Charla)

Feminine of the Old Norse Carl, meaning 'free man'.

Carlin

(alt. Carleen, Carlene)

Gaelic, meaning 'little champion'.

Carlotta

(alt. Carlota)

Italian form of Charlotte, meaning 'little and feminine'.

Carly

(alt. Carlee, Carley, Carli, Carlie)

Feminine of the German Charles, meaning 'free man'.

Carmel

(alt. Carmela, Carmelita, Carmella)

Hebrew, meaning 'garden'.

Carmen

(alt. Carma, Carmina)

Latin, meaning 'song'.

Carol

(alt. Carole, Carrol, Carroll, Caryl)

Shortened form of Caroline, meaning 'man'.

Caroline

(alt. Carolann, Carolina, Carolyn, Carolynn)

German, meaning 'man'.

Carrington

English, meaning 'Charles's town'.

Carys

(alt. Cerys)

Welsh, meaning 'love'.

Casey

Irish Gaelic, meaning 'watchful'.

C

Saints' names

Agatha
Agnes
Barbara
Cecilia
Genevieve
Louise
Matilda
Seraphina
Tatiana
Teresa
Vivian

Cassandra
(alt. Casandra, Cassandre)
Greek, meaning 'one who prophesies doom'.

Cassia
(alt. Casia, Casie, Cassie)
Greek, meaning 'cinnamon'.

Cassidy
Irish, meaning 'clever'.

Cassiopeia
(alt. Cassiopia, Cassiopea)
Greek, from the constellation and the Greek myth.

Catalina
(alt. Catarina, Caterina)
Spanish version of Catherine, meaning 'pure'.

Catherine
(alt. Catharine, Cathrine, Cathryn)
Greek, meaning 'pure'.

Cathleen
Irish version of Catherine, meaning 'pure'.

Cathy
(alt. Cathey, Cathi, Cathie)
Shortened form of Catherine, meaning 'pure'.

Caty
(alt. Caddie, Caitee, Cate, Catie)
Shortened form of Catherine, meaning 'pure'.

Cayley
(alt. Cayla, Caylee, Caylen)
American, meaning 'pure'.

Cecile
(alt. Cecilie)
Latin, meaning 'blind one'.

C

Cecilia
(alt. Cecelia, Cecily, Cicely, Cicily)
Latin, meaning 'blind one'.

Celena
Greek, meaning 'goddess of the moon'.

Celeste
(alt. Celestina, Celestine)
Latin, meaning 'heavenly'.

Celine
(alt. Celia, Celina)
French version of Celeste, meaning 'heavenly'.

Cerise
French, meaning 'cherry'.

Chanah
Hebrew, meaning 'grace'.

Chandler
(alt. Chandell)
English, meaning 'candle maker'.

Chandra
(alt. Chanda, Chandry)
Sanskrit, meaning 'like the moon'.

Chanel
(alt. Chanelle)
French, meaning 'pipe'. Most often associated with the designer of the same name.

Chantal
(alt. Chantel, Chantelle, Chantilly)
French, meaning 'stony spot'.

Chardonnay
French, from the wine variety of the same name.

Charis
(alt. Charissa, Charisse)
Greek, meaning 'grace'.

Charity
Latin, meaning 'brotherly love'.

Charlene
(alt. Charleen, Charline)
German, meaning 'man'.

Charlie
(alt. Charlee, Charley Charlize, Charly)
Shortened form of Charlotte, meaning 'little and feminine'.

229

Charlotte
(alt. Charnette, Charolette)

French, meaning 'little and feminine'.

Charmaine
Latin, meaning 'clan'.

Charnelle
(alt. Charnell, Charnel, Charnele)

American, meaning 'sparkles'.

Chastity
Latin, meaning 'purity'.

Chava
(alt. Chaya)

Hebrew, meaning 'beloved'.

Chelsea
(alt. Chelsee, Chelsey, Chelsi, Chelsie)

English, meaning 'port or landing place'.

Cher
French, meaning 'beloved'. Most often associated with the singer of the same name.

Cherie
(alt. Cheri, Cherise)

French, meaning 'dear'.

Cherish
(alt. Cherith)

English, meaning 'to treasure'.

Chermona
Hebrew, meaning 'sacred mountain'.

Cherry
(alt. Cherri)

French, meaning 'cherry fruit'.

TV personality names

Alexa (Chung)
Alesha (Dixon)
Cheryl (Cole)
Dannii (Minogue)
Davina (McCall)
Fearne (Cotton)
Holly (Willoughby)
Kirsty (Alsopp)
Myleene (Klass)
Natasha (Kaplinsky)
Tess (Daly)
Trisha (Goddard)

C

Cheryl
(alt. Cheryle)
English, meaning 'little and womanly'.

Chesney
English, meaning 'place to camp'.

Cheyenne
(alt. Cheyanne)
Native American, from the tribe of the same name.

Chiara
(alt. Ceara, Chiarina, Ciara)
Italian, meaning 'light'.

China
From the country of the same name.

Chiquita
Spanish, meaning 'little one'.

Chloe
(alt. Cloe)
Greek, meaning 'pale green shoot'.

Chloris
Greek, meaning 'pale'.

Chris
(alt. Chrissy, Christa, Christie, Christy, Crissy, Cristy)
Shortened form of Christina, meaning 'anointed Christian'.

Christabel
Latin and French, meaning 'fair Christian'. The title of a poem by Coleridge.

Christina
(alt. Christiana, Cristina)
Greek, meaning 'anointed Christian'.

Christine
(alt. Christeen, Christene, Christiane, Christin)
Greek, meaning 'anointed Christian'.

Chuma
Aramaic, meaning 'warmth'.

Ciara
Irish, meaning 'dark beauty'.

Cierra
(alt. Ciera)
Irish, meaning 'black'.

C

Cinderella

French, meaning 'little ash-girl'. Most often associated with the fairytale.

Cindy

(alt. Cinda, Cindi, Cyndi)

Shortened form of Cynthia, meaning 'goddess'.

Cinnamon

Greek, from the spice of the same name.

Citlali

(alt. Citlalli)

Aztec, meaning 'star'.

Citrine

Latin, from the gemstone of the same name.

Claire

(alt. Clare)

Latin, meaning 'bright'.

Clara

(alt. Claira)

Latin, meaning 'bright'.

Clarabelle

(alt. Claribel)

Contraction of Clara and Isobel, meaning 'bright' and 'consecrated to God'.

Clarissa

(alt. Clarice, Clarisse)

Variation of Claire, meaning 'bright'.

Clarity

Latin, meaning 'lucid'.

Claudette

Latin, meaning 'lame'.

Claudia

(alt. Claudie, Claudine)

Latin, meaning 'lame'.

Clematis

Greek, meaning 'vine'.

Clementine

(alt. Clemency, Clementina, Clemmie)

Latin, meaning 'mild and merciful'.

Cleopatra

Greek, meaning 'her father's renown'. Most often associated with the Egyptian queen.

Clio
(alt. Cleo, Cliona)

Greek, from the muse of history of the same name.

Clodagh
Irish, meaning 'river'.

Clotilda
(alt. Clothilda, Clothilde, Clotilde)

German, meaning 'renowned battle'.

Clover
English, from the flower of the same name.

Cloud
American, meaning 'lighthearted'.

Coco
Spanish, meaning 'help'.

Cody
English, meaning 'pillow'.

Colleen
(alt. Coleen)

Irish Gaelic, meaning 'girl'.

Collette
(alt. Colette)

Greek and French, meaning 'people of victory'.

Connie
Latin, meaning 'steadfast'.

Constance
(alt. Constanza)

Latin, meaning 'steadfast'.

Consuelo
(alt. Consuela)

Spanish, meaning 'comfort'.

Cora
Greek, meaning 'maiden'.

Coral
(alt. Coralie, Coraline, Corelia, Corene)

Latin, from the marine life of the same name.

Corazon
Spanish, meaning 'heart'.

Cordelia
(alt. Cordia, Cordie)

Latin, meaning 'heart'.

C

Corey
(alt. Cori, Corrie, Cory)
Irish Gaelic, meaning 'the hollow'.

Corin
(alt. Corine)
Latin, meaning 'spear'.

Corinne
(alt. Corinna, Corrine)
French version of Cora, meaning 'maiden'.

Corliss
English, meaning 'cheery'.

Cornelia
Latin, meaning 'like a horn'.

Cosette
French, meaning 'people of victory'.

Cosima
(alt. Cosmina)
Greek, meaning 'order'.

Courtney
(alt. Cortney)
English, meaning 'court-dweller'.

Creola
French, meaning 'American-born, English descent'.

Crescent
French, meaning 'increasing'.

Cressida
From the heroine in Greek mythology of the same name.

Crystal
(alt. Christal, Chrystal, Cristal)
Greek, meaning 'ice'.

Csilla
Hungarian, meaning 'defences'.

Cynara
Greek, meaning 'thistly plant'.

Cynthia
Greek, meaning 'goddess from the mountain'.

Cyra
Persian, meaning 'sun'.

Cyrilla
Latin, meaning 'lordly'.

 Girls' names

Dacey

Irish Gaelic, meaning 'from the south'.

Dada

Nigerian, meaning 'curly haired'.

Daelan

English, meaning 'aware'.

Dagmar

German, meaning 'day's glory'.

Dagny

Nordic, meaning 'new day'.

Dahlia

Scandinavian, from the flower of the same name.

Dai

Japanese, meaning 'great'.

Daisy

(alt. Dasia)

English, meaning 'eye of the day'.

Dakota

Native American, meaning 'allies'.

Dalia

(alt. Dalila)

Hebrew, meaning 'delicate branch'.

Dallas

Scottish Gaelic, from the village of the same name. Also a city in the USA.

D

Damaris

Greek, meaning 'calf'.

Damica

(alt. Damika)

French, meaning 'friendly'.

Damita

Spanish, meaning 'little noblewoman'.

Dana

(alt. Dania, Danna, Dayna)

English, meaning 'from Denmark'.

Danae

Greek, from the mythological heroine of the same name.

Danica

(alt. Danika)

Latin, meaning 'from Denmark'.

Danielle

(alt. Danelle, Daniela, Daniella, Danila, Danyelle)

The feminine form of the Hebrew Daniel, meaning 'God is my judge'.

Danita

English, meaning 'God will judge'.

Daphne

(alt. Dafne, Daphna)

Greek, meaning 'laurel tree'.

Dara

Hebrew and Persian, meaning 'wisdom'.

Darby

(alt. Darbi, Darbie)

Irish, meaning 'park with deer'.

Darcie

(alt. Darci, Darcy)

Irish Gaelic, meaning 'dark'.

Daria

Greek, meaning 'rich'.

Darla

English, meaning 'darling'.

Darlene

(alt. Darleen, Darline)

American, meaning 'darling'.

Darva

Slavic, meaning 'honeybee'.

Daryl
(alt. Darryl)

English, originally used as a surname. Often associated with the actress Daryl Hannah.

Davina

Hebrew, meaning 'loved one'. Best known for the TV presenter Davina McCall.

Dawn
(alt. Dawna)

English, meaning 'the dawn'.

Daya

Hebrew, meaning 'bird of prey'.

Deanna
(alt. Dayana, Deana, Deanna, Deanne)

English, meaning 'valley'.

Debbie
(alt. Debbi, Debby, Debi)

Shortened form of Deborah, meaning 'bee'.

Deborah
(alt. Debbra, Debora, Debra, Debrah)

Hebrew, meaning 'bee'.

December

Latin, meaning 'tenth month'.

Decima
(alt. Decia)

Latin, meaning 'tenth'.

Dee

Welsh, meaning 'swarthy'.

Deidre
(alt. Deidra, Deirdre)

Irish, meaning 'raging woman'.

Deja
(alt. Dejah)

French, meaning 'already'.

Delaney

Irish Gaelic, meaning 'offspring of the challenger'.

Delia

Greek, meaning 'from Delos'.

Delilah
(alt. Delina)

Hebrew, meaning 'seductive'.

Della
(alt. Dell)

Shortened form of Adele, meaning 'nobility'.

D

Delores
(alt. Deloris)
Spanish, meaning 'sorrows'.

Delphine
(alt. Delpha, Delphia, Delphina, Delphinia)
Greek, meaning 'dolphin'.

Delta
Greek, meaning 'fourth child'.

Demetria
(alt. Demetrice, Dimitria)
Greek, from the mythological heroine of the same name.

Demi
French, meaning 'half'. Best known for the actress Demi Moore.

Dena
(alt. Deena)
English, meaning 'from the valley'.

Denise
(alt. Denice, Denisa, Denisse)
French, meaning 'follower of Dionysius'.

Derora
Hebrew, meaning 'stream'.

Desdemona
Greek, meaning 'wretchedness'.

Desiree
(alt. Desirae)
French, meaning 'much desired'.

Desma
Greek, meaning 'blinding oath'.

Destiny
(alt. Destany, Destinee, Destiney, Destini)
French, meaning 'fate'.

Deva
Hindi, meaning 'God-like'.

Devin
(alt. Devinne)
Irish Gaelic, meaning 'poet'.

Devon
English, from the county of the same name.

Diamond
English, meaning 'brilliant'.

Diana
(alt. Dian, Diane, Dianna, Dianne)
Roman, meaning 'divine'.

D

Uncommon three-syllable names

Annabel
Cassandra
Dolores
Gloria
Harriet
Imogen
Julia
Marilyn
Miranda
Nigella

Diandra
Greek, meaning 'two males'.

Dilys
Welsh, meaning 'reliable'.

Dimona
Hebrew, meaning 'south'.

Dinah
(alt. Dina)
Hebrew, meaning 'justified'.

Dionne
Greek, from the mythological heroine of the same name.

Divine
Italian, meaning 'heavenly'.

Dixie
French, meaning 'tenth'.

Dodie
Hebrew, meaning 'well-loved'.

Dolly
(alt. Dollie)
Shortened form of Dorothy, meaning 'gift of God'.

Dolores
(alt. Doloris)
Spanish, meaning 'sorrows'.

Dominique
(alt. Domenica, Dominica, Domonique)
Latin, meaning 'Lord'.

Donata
Latin, meaning 'given'.

Donna
(alt. Dona, Donnie)
Italian, meaning 'lady'.

Dora
Greek, meaning 'gift'.

Dorcas
Greek, meaning 'gazelle'.

Doreen
(alt. Dorene, Dorine)
Irish Gaelic, meaning 'brooding'.

Doria
Greek, meaning 'of the sea'.

Doris
(alt. Dorris)
Greek, from the region of the same name.

Dorothy
(alt. Dorathy, Doretha, Dorotha, Dorothea, Dorthy)
Greek, meaning 'gift of God'.

Dorrit
(alt. Dorit)
Greek, meaning 'gift of God'.

Dory
(alt. Dori)
French, meaning 'gilded'.

Dottie
(alt. Dotty)
Shortened form of Dorothy, meaning 'gift of God'.

Dove
(alt. Dovie)
English, from the bird of the same name.

Drew
Greek, meaning 'masculine'.

Drusilla
(alt. Drucilla)
Latin, meaning 'of the Drusus clan'.

Dulcie
(alt. Dulce, Dulcia)
Latin, meaning 'sweet'.

Dusty
(alt. Dusti)
Old German, meaning 'brave warrior'. Often associated with the singer Dusty Springfield.

D

E Girls' names

Eadlin
(alt. Eadlinn, Eadlyn, Eadlen)
Anglo-Saxon, meaning 'royalty'.

Earla
English, meaning 'leader'.

Eartha
English, meaning 'earth'.

Easter
Egyptian, from the festival of the same name.

Ebba
English, meaning 'fortress of riches'.

Ebony
(alt. Eboni)
Latin, meaning 'deep black wood'.

Echo
Greek, meaning 'reflected sound'. From the mythological nymph of the same name.

Eda
(alt. Edda)
English, meaning 'wealthy and happy'.

Edelmira
Spanish, meaning 'admired for nobility'.

Eden
Hebrew, meaning 'pleasure'.

Edie
(alt. Eddie)
Shortened form of Eden, meaning 'pleasure'.

Edina

Scottish, meaning 'from Edinburgh'.

Edith

(alt. Edyth)

English, meaning 'prosperity through battle'.

Edna

Hebrew, meaning 'enjoyment'.

Edrea

English, meaning 'wealthy and powerful'.

Edris

(alt. Edriss, Edrys)

Anglo-Saxon, meaning 'prosperous ruler'.

Edwina

English, meaning 'wealthy friend'.

Effie

Greek, meaning 'pleasant speech'.

Eglantine

French, from the shrub of the same name.

Eibhlín

Irish Gaelic, meaning 'shining and brilliant'.

Eileen

Irish, meaning 'shining and brilliant'.

Ekaterina

(alt. Ekaterini)

Slavic, meaning 'pure'.

Elaine

(alt. Elaina, Elayne)

French, meaning 'bright, shining light'.

Elba

Italian, from the island of the same name.

Elberta

English, meaning 'highborn'.

Eldora

Spanish, meaning 'covered with gold'.

Eldoris

(alt. Eldoriss, Eldorys)

Greek, meaning 'woman of the sea'.

Eleanor

(alt. Elana, Elanor, Eleanora)

Greek, meaning 'light'.

Electra
(alt. Elektra)
Greek, meaning 'shining'. Also from the myth.

Elfrida
(alt. Elfrieda)
English, meaning 'elf power'.

Eliane
Hebrew, meaning 'Jehovah is God'.

Elissa
(alt. Elisa)
French, meaning 'pledged to God'.

Eliza
(alt. Elisha)
Hebrew, meaning 'consecrated to God'.

Elizabeth
(alt. Elisabet, Elisabeth, Elizabella, Elizabelle, Elsbeth, Elspeth)
Hebrew, meaning 'consecrated to God'.

Elke
German, meaning 'nobility'.

Ella
German, meaning 'completely'.

Elle
(alt. Ellie)
French, meaning 'she'.

Ellema
(alt. Ellemah, Elema, Ellemma, Elemah)
African, meaning 'dairy farmer'.

Ellen
(alt. Elin, Eline, Ellyn)
Greek, meaning 'shining'.

Ellice
(alt. Elyse)
Greek, meaning 'the Lord is God'.

Elma
(alt. Elna)
Latin, meaning 'soul'.

Elmira
Arabic, meaning 'aristocratic lady'.

Elodie
French, meaning 'marsh flower'.

Eloise
(alt. Elois, Eloisa, Elouise)
French, meaning 'renowned in battle'.

Elsa
(alt. Else, Elsie)
Hebrew, meaning 'consecrated to God'.

Elva
Irish, meaning 'noble'.

Elvina
English, meaning 'noble friend'.

Elvira
(alt. Elvera)
Spanish, from the ancient city of the same name.

Ember
(alt. Embry)
English, meaning 'spark'.

Emeline
German, meaning 'industrious'.

Emerald
English, meaning 'green gemstone'.

Emery
German, meaning 'ruler of work'.

Emiko
(alt. Emuko)
Japanese, meaning 'pretty child'.

Emilia
Latin, meaning 'rival, eager'.

Emily
(alt. Emalee, Emelie, Emely, Emilee, Emilie, Emlyn)
Latin, meaning 'rival, eager'.

Emma
German, meaning 'embraces everything'. The title character of Jane Austen's novel.

Emmanuelle
Hebrew, meaning 'God is among us'.

Emmeline
(alt. Emmelina)
German, meaning 'embraces everything'.

Emmy
(alt. Emi, Emme, Emmie)
German, meaning 'embraces everything'.

Ena
Shortened form of Georgina, meaning 'farmer'.

Enid
(alt. Eneida)
Welsh, meaning 'life spirit'.

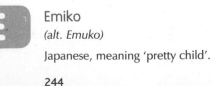

Enola
Native American, meaning 'solitary'.

Enya
Irish Gaelic, meaning 'fire'.

Eranthe
Greek, meaning 'delicate like the spring'.

Erica
(alt. Ericka, Erika)
Scandinavian, meaning 'ruler forever'.

Erin
(alt. Eryn)
Irish Gaelic, meaning 'from the isle to the west'.

Eris
Greek, from the mythological heroine of the same name.

Erlinda
Hebrew, meaning 'spirited'.

Erma
German, meaning 'universal'.

Ermine
French, meaning 'weasel'.

Erna
English, meaning 'sincere'.

Ernestine
(alt. Ernestina)
English, meaning 'sincere'.

Esme
French, meaning 'esteemed'.

Esmeralda
Spanish, meaning 'emerald'.

Esperanza
Spanish, meaning 'hope'.

Estelle
(alt. Estela, Estell, Estella)
French, meaning 'star'.

Esther
(alt. Esta, Ester, Etha, Ethna, Ethne)
Persian, meaning 'star'.

Etinia
(alt. Eteniah, Etene, Eteniya)
Native American, meaning 'prosperous'.

Eternity
Latin, meaning 'forever'.

E

245

Ethel
(alt. Ethyl)
English, meaning 'noble'.

Etta
(alt. Etter, Ettie)
Shortened form of Henrietta, meaning 'ruler of the house'.

Eudora
Greek, meaning 'generous gift'.

Eugenia
(alt. Eugenie)
Greek, meaning 'well born'.

Eulalia
(alt. Eula, Eulah, Eulalie)
Greek, meaning 'sweet-speaking'.

Eunice
Greek, meaning 'victorious'.

Euphemia
Greek, meaning ' favourable speech'.

Eva
Hebrew, meaning 'life'.

Evadne
Greek, meaning 'pleasing one'.

Evangeline
(alt. Evangelina)
Greek, meaning 'good news'.

Evanthe
Greek, meaning 'good flower'.

Eve
(alt. Evie)
Hebrew, meaning 'life'. The first woman created by God in the Bible.

Evelina
(alt. Evelia)
German, meaning 'hazelnut'.

Evelyn
(alt. Evalyn, Evelin, Eveline, Evelyne)
German, meaning 'hazelnut'.

Everly
(alt. Everleigh, Everley)
English, meaning 'grazing meadow'.

Evette
French, meaning 'yew wood'.

Evonne
(alt. Evon)
French, meaning 'yew wood'.

F

Girls' names

Fabia
(alt. Fabiana, Fabienne, Fabiola, Fabriana)
Latin, meaning 'from the Fabian clan'.

Fabrizia
Italian, meaning 'works with hands'.

Fahari
Swahili, meaning 'splendour'.

Faith
English, meaning 'loyalty'.

Faiza
Arabic, meaning 'victorious'.

Fallon
Irish Gaelic, meaning 'descended from a ruler'.

Fanny
(alt Fannie)
Latin, meaning 'from France'.

Farica
German, meaning 'peaceful ruler'.

Farrah
English, meaning 'lovely and pleasant'.

Fatima
Arabic, meaning 'baby's nurse'.

Faustine
Latin, meaning 'fortunate'.

Fawn
French, meaning 'young deer'.

Fay
(alt. Fae, Faye)
French, meaning 'fairy'.

Fayola
(alt. Fayolah, Fayeena)
African, meaning 'walks with honour'.

Felicia
(alt. Felecia, Felice, Felicita, Felisha)
Latin, meaning 'lucky and happy'.

Felicity
Latin, meaning 'fortunate'.

Fenella
Irish Gaelic, meaning 'white shoulder'.

Fenia
Scandinavian, from the mythological giantess of the same name.

Fern
(alt. Ferne, Ferrin)
English, from the plant of the same name.

Fernanda
German, meaning 'peace and courage'.

Ffion
(alt. Fion)
Irish Gaelic, meaning 'fair and pale'.

Old name, new fashion?

Arabella
Clara
Clarissa
Dorothy
Evelyn
Hazel
Marjorie
Nora
Penelope
Rosamond

F

Fia

Italian, meaning 'flame'.

Fifi

Hebrew, meaning 'Jehovah increases'.

Filomena

Greek, meaning 'loved one'.

Finlay

(alt. Finley)

Irish Gaelic, meaning 'fair-headed courageous one'.

Finola

(alt. Fionnula)

Irish Gaelic, meaning 'fair shoulder'.

Fiona

Irish Gaelic, meaning 'fair and pale'.

Fiora

Irish Gaelic, meaning 'fair and pale'.

Fiorella

Italian, meaning 'little flower'.

Flanna

(alt. Flannery)

Irish Gaelic, meaning 'russet hair'.

Flavia

Latin, meaning 'yellow hair'.

Fleur

French, meaning 'flower'.

Flo

(alt. Florrie, Flossie, Floy)

Shortened form of Florence, meaning 'in bloom'.

Flora

Latin, meaning 'flower'.

Florence

(alt. Florencia, Florene, Florine)

Latin, meaning 'in bloom'. Also the Italian city.

Florida

Latin, meaning 'flowery'. Also a state in the USA.

Fran

(alt. Frankie, Frannie)

Shortened form of Frances, meaning 'from France'.

F

Frances
(alt. Francine, Francis)
Latin, meaning 'from France'.

Francesca
(alt. Franchesca, Francisca)
Latin, meaning 'from France'.

Freda
(alt. Freeda, Freida, Frida, Frieda)
German, meaning 'peaceful'.

Frederica
German, meaning 'peaceful ruler'.

Fuchsia
German, from the flower of the same name.

Fumik
Japanese, meaning 'little friend'.

Names of poets

Amy (Lowell)
Anne (Sexton)
Carol Ann (Duffy)
Charlotte (Smith)
Emily (Dickinson)
Fleur (Adcock)
Gwyneth (Lewis)
Ruth (Padel)
Pam (Ayres)
Sylvia (Plath)
Wendy (Cope)

F

Girls' names

Gabby
(alt. Gabbi)
Shortened form of Gabrielle, meaning 'heroine of God'.

Gabrielle
(alt. Gabriel, Gabriela, Gabriella)
Hebrew, meaning 'heroine of God'.

Gadara
Armenian, meaning 'mountain's peak'.

Gaia
(alt. Gaea)
Greek, meaning 'the earth'.

Gail
(alt. Gale, Gayla, Gayle)
Hebrew, meaning 'my father rejoices'.

Gala
French, meaning 'festive merrymaking'.

Galiena
German, meaning 'high one'.

Galina
Russian, meaning 'shining brightly'.

Garnet
(alt. Garnett)
English, meaning 'red gemstone'.

Gay
(alt. Gaye)
French, meaning 'glad and lighthearted'.

Gaynor

Welsh, meaning 'white and smooth'.

Gemini

Greek, meaning 'twin'. One of the signs of the zodiac.

Gemma

Italian, meaning 'precious stone'.

Gene

Greek, meaning 'wellborn'.

Genesis

Greek, meaning 'beginning'.

Geneva

(alt. Genevra)

French, meaning 'juniper tree'.

Genevieve

German, meaning 'white wave'.

Genie

Shortened form of Genevieve, meaning 'white wave'.

Georgette

French, meaning 'farmer'.

Names from ancient Rome

Agnes
Cecilia
Chloris
Diana
Flavia
Lavinia
Octavia
Paula
Portia
Tatiana

Georgia

(alt. Georgiana, Georgianna, Georgie)

Latin, meaning 'farmer'.

Georgina

(alt. Georgene, Georgine, Giorgina)

Latin, meaning 'farmer'.

Geraldine

German, meaning 'spear ruler'.

Gerda

Nordic, meaning 'shelter'.

G

Geri
(alt. Gerri, Gerry)
Shortened form of Geraldine, meaning 'spear ruler'.

Germaine
French, meaning 'from Germany'.

Gertie
Shortened form of Gertrude, meaning 'strength of a spear'.

Gertrude
German, meaning 'strength of a spear'.

Ghislaine
French, meaning 'pledge'.

Gia
(alt. Ghia)
Italian, meaning 'God is gracious'.

Gianina
(alt. Giana)
Hebrew, meaning 'God's graciousness'.

Gigi
(alt. Giget)
Shortened form of Georgina, meaning 'farmer'.

Gilda
English, meaning 'gilded'.

Gilia
Hebrew, meaning 'joy of the Lord'.

Gillian
Latin, meaning 'youthful'.

Gina
(alt. Geena, Gena)
Shortened form of Regina, meaning 'queen'.

Ginger
Latin, from the root of the same name.

Ginny
Shortened form of Virginia, meaning 'virgin'.

Giovanna
Italian, meaning 'God is gracious'.

Giselle
(alt. Gisela, Gisele, Giselle, Gisselle)
German, meaning 'pledge'.

Gita
(alt. Geeta)
Sanskrit, meaning 'song'.

Giulia
(alt. Giuliana)
Italian, meaning 'youthful'.

Gladys
(alt. Gladyce)
Welsh, meaning 'lame'.

Glenda
Welsh, meaning 'fair and good'.

Glenna
(alt. Glennie)
Irish Gaelic, meaning 'glen'.

Glenys
Welsh, meaning 'riverbank'.

Gloria
(alt. Glory)
Latin, meaning 'glory'.

Glynda
(alt. Glinda)
Welsh, meaning 'fair'. The good witch in the *Wizard of Oz*.

Glynis
Welsh, meaning 'small glen'.

Golda
(alt. Goldia, Goldie)
English, meaning 'gold'.

Grace
(alt. Graça, Gracie, Gracin, Grayce)
Latin, meaning 'grace'.

Grainne
(alt. Grania)
Irish Gaelic, meaning 'love'.

Gratia
(alt. Grasia)
Latin, meaning 'blessing'.

Greer
(alt. Grier)
Latin, meaning 'alert and watchful'.

Gregoria
Latin, meaning 'alert'.

Greta
(alt. Gretel)
Greek, meaning 'pearl'.

G

Gretchen
German, meaning 'pearl'.

Griselda
(alt. Griselle)
German, meaning 'grey fighting maid'.

Gudrun
Scandinavian, meaning 'battle'.

Guinevere
Welsh, meaning 'white and smooth'. The queen in Arthurian legend.

Gwen
Shortened form of Gwendolyn, meaning 'fair bow'.

Gwenda
Welsh, meaning 'fair and good'.

Gwendolyn
(alt. Gwendolen, Gwenel)
Welsh, meaning 'fair bow'.

Gwyneth
(alt. Gwynneth, Gwynyth)
Welsh, meaning 'happiness'.

Gwynn
(alt. Gwyn)
Welsh, meaning 'fair blessed'.

Gypsy
English, meaning 'of the Roman tribe'.

Grythao
English, meaning 'fiery'.

Names from ancient Greece

Agatha
Ariadne
Berenice
Cressida
Iliana
Lisandra
Medea
Nereida
Sophia
Xenia

G

255

English and Scottish royalty

Anna	Mairi
Anne	Margaret
Catherine	Mary
Eleanor	Matilda
Elizabeth	Victoria

G

Girls' names

Habibah
(alt. Habiba)
Arabic, meaning 'beloved'.

Hadassah
Hebrew, meaning 'myrtle tree'.

Hadley
English, meaning 'heather meadow'.

Hadria
Latin, meaning 'from Adria'.

Hala
Arabic, meaning 'halo'.

Haley
(alt. Haelee, Haely, Hailee, Hailey, Hailie, Haleigh, Hali, Halie)
English, meaning 'hay meadow'.

Halima
(alt. Halina)
Arabic, meaning 'gentle'.

Hallie
(alt. Halle, Halley, Hallie)
German, meaning 'ruler of the home or estate'.

Hannah
(alt. Haana, Hana, Hanna)
Hebrew, meaning 'grace'.

Harika
Turkish, meaning 'superior one'.

Harley
(alt. Harlene)
English, meaning 'the long field'.

Harlow
English, meaning 'army hill'.

Harmony
Latin, meaning 'harmony'.

Harper
English, meaning 'minstrel'.

Harriet
(alt. Harriett, Harriette)
German, meaning 'ruler of the home or estate'.

Hattie
Shortened form of Harriet, meaning 'ruler of the home or estate'.

Haven
English, meaning 'a place of sanctuary'.

Hayden
Old English, meaning 'hedged valley'.

Hayley
(alt. Haylee, Hayleigh, Haylie)
English, meaning 'hay meadow'.

Hazel
(alt. Hazle)
English, from the tree of the same name.

Heather
English, from the flower of the same name.

Heaven
English, meaning 'everlasting bliss'.

Hedda
German, meaning 'warfare'.

Hedwig
German, meaning 'warfare and strife'.

Heidi
(alt. Heidy)
German, meaning 'nobility'.

Helen
(alt. Halen, Helena, Helene, Hellen)
Greek, meaning 'light'.

Helga
German, meaning 'holy and sacred'.

Helia
Greek, meaning 'sun'.

Heloise
French, meaning 'renowned in war'.

Henrietta
(alt. Henriette)
German, meaning 'ruler of the house'.

Hephzibah
Hebrew, meaning 'my delight is in her'.

Hera
Greek, meaning 'queen'. The wife of Zeus in Greek mythology.

Hermia
(alt. Hermina, Hermine, Herminia)
Greek, meaning 'messenger'.

Hermione
Greek, meaning 'earthly'. Best known for the Harry Potter character.

Hero
Greek, meaning 'brave one of the people'.

Hertha
English, meaning 'earth'.

Hesper
(alt. Hesperia)
Greek, meaning 'evening star'.

Hester
(alt. Hestia)
Greek, meaning 'star'.

Hilary
(alt. Hillary)
Greek, meaning 'cheerful and happy'.

Hilda
(alt. Hildur)
German, meaning 'battle woman'.

Hildegarde
(alt. Hildegard)

German, meaning 'battle stronghold'.

Hildred

German, meaning 'battle counsellor'.

Hilma

German variant of Wilhelmina, meaning 'helmet'.

Hirkani

Indian, meaning 'like a diamond'.

Hollis

English, meaning 'near the holly bushes'.

Holly
(alt. Holli, Hollie)

English, from the tree of the same name.

Honey

English, meaning 'honey'.

Honor
(alt. Honour)

Latin, meaning 'woman of honour'.

Honora
(alt. Honoria)

Latin, meaning 'woman of honour'.

Hope

English, meaning 'hope'.

Hortense
(alt. Hortencia, Hortensia)

Latin, meaning 'of the garden'.

Hudson

English, meaning 'adventurous'.

Hulda

German, meaning 'loved one'.

Hyacinth

Greek, from the flower of the same name.

Girls' names

Iantha
Greek, meaning 'purple flower'.

Ichigo
Japanese, meaning 'strawberry'.

Ida
English, meaning 'prosperous'.

Idell
(alt. Idella)
English, meaning 'prosperous'.

Idona
Nordic, meaning 'renewal'.

Ignacia
Latin, meaning 'ardent'.

Ila
French, meaning 'island'.

Ilana
Hebrew, meaning 'tree'.

Ilaria
Italian, meaning 'cheerful'.

Ilene
American, meaning 'light'.

Iliana
(alt. Ileana)
Greek, meaning 'Trojan'.

Ilona
Hungarian, meaning 'light'.

Ilsa

German, meaning 'pledged to God'.

Ima

German, meaning 'embraces everything'.

Iman

Arabic, meaning 'faith'.

Imara

Hungarian, meaning 'great ruler'.

Imelda

German, meaning 'all-consuming fight'.

Imogen
(alt. Imogene)

Latin, meaning 'last-born'.

Ina

Latin, meaning 'to make feminine'.

Inaya

Arabic, meaning 'taking care'.

India
(alt. Indie)

Hindi, from the country of the same name.

Indiana

Latin, meaning 'from India'. Also a state in the USA.

Indigo

Greek, meaning 'deep blue dye'.

Indira
(alt. Inira)

Sanskrit, meaning 'beauty'.

Inez
(alt. Ines)

Spanish, meaning 'pure'.

Inga
(alt. Inge, Ingeborg, Inger)

Scandinavian, meaning 'guarded by Ing'.

Ingrid

Scandinavian, meaning 'beautiful'.

Io
(alt. Eyo)

Greek, from the mythological heroine of the same name.

I

Ioanna
Greek, meaning 'grace'.

Iola
(alt. Iole)
Greek, meaning 'cloud of dawn'.

Iolanthe
Greek, meaning 'violet flower'.

Iona
Greek, from the island of the same name.

Ione
Greek, meaning 'violet'.

Iorwen
Welsh, meaning 'fair'.

Iphigenia
Greek, meaning 'sacrifice'.

Ira
(alt. Iva)
Hebrew, meaning 'watchful'.

Irene
(alt. Irelyn, Irena, Irina, Irini)
Greek, meaning 'peace'.

Iris
Greek, meaning 'rainbow'. Also from the flower of the same name.

Irma
German, meaning 'universal'.

Isabel
(alt. Isabela, Isabell, Isabella, Isabelle, Isabeth, Isobel, Izabella, Izabelle)
Spanish, meaning 'pledged to God'.

Isadora
Latin, meaning 'gift of Isis'.

Ishana
Hindi, meaning 'desire'.

Isis
Egyptian, from the goddess of the same name.

Isla
(alt. Isa, Isela, Isley)
Scottish Gaelic, meaning 'river'.

Isolde
Welsh, meaning 'fair lady'.

Istas

Native American, meaning 'snow'.

Ivana

Slavic, meaning 'Jehovah is gracious'.

Ivette

Variation of Yvette, meaning 'yew wood'.

Ivonne

Variation of Yvonne, meaning 'yew wood'.

Ivory

Latin, meaning 'white as elephant tusks'.

Ivy

English, from the plant of the same name.

Ixia

South African, from the flower of the same name.

Boys' names for girls (female spellings)

Alex
Billie
Cori
Charlie
Elliott
Geri
Jamie
Jo
Leslie
Robyn
Toni

J Girls' names

Jaamini
Hindi, meaning 'evening'.

Jacinda
(alt. Jacinta)
Spanish, meaning 'hyacinth'.

Jackie
(alt. Jacque, Jacqui)
Shortened form of Jacqueline, meaning 'he who supplants'.

Jacqueline
(alt. Jacalyn, Jacklyn, Jaclyn, Jacquelin, Jacquelyn, Jacquline, Jaqlyn, Jaquelin, Jaqueline)
French, meaning 'he who supplants'.

Jade
(alt. Jada, Jaida, Jayda, Jayde)
Spanish, meaning 'green stone'.

Jaden
(alt. Jadyn, Jaiden, Jaidyn, Jayden)
Contraction of Jade and Hayden, meaning 'green hedged valley'.

Jael
Hebrew, meaning 'mountain goat'.

Jaime
(alt. Jaima, Jaimie, Jami, Jamie)
Spanish, meaning 'he who supplants'.

Jamila
Arabic, meaning 'lovely'.

Jan
(alt. Jann, Janna)

Hebrew, meaning 'the Lord is gracious'.

Jana
(alt. Jaana)

Hebrew, meaning 'the Lord is gracious'.

Janae
(alt. Janay)

American, meaning 'the Lord is gracious'.

Jane
(alt. Jayne)

Feminine form of the Hebrew John, meaning 'the Lord is gracious'.

Janelle
(alt. Janel, Janell, Jenelle)

American, meaning 'the Lord is gracious'.

Janet
(alt. Janette)

Scottish, meaning 'the Lord is gracious'.

Janice
(alt. Janis)

American, meaning 'the Lord is gracious'.

Janie
(alt. Janney, Jannie)

Shortened form of Janet, meaning 'the Lord is gracious'.

Janine
(alt. Janeen)

English, meaning 'the Lord is gracious'.

Janoah
(alt. Janiya, Janiyah)

Hebrew, meaning 'quiet and calm'.

January

Latin, meaning 'the first month'.

Jarita

Hindi-Sanskrit, meaning 'famous bird'.

Jasmine
(alt. Jasmin, Jazim, Jazmine)

Persian, meaning 'jasmine flower'.

J

Jay

Latin, meaning 'jaybird'.

Jayna

Sanskrit, meaning 'bringer of victory'.

Jean

(alt. Jeane, Jeanne)

Scottish, meaning 'the Lord is gracious'.

Jeana

(alt. Jeanna)

Latin, meaning 'queen'.

Jeanette

(alt. Jeannette, Janette)

French, meaning 'the Lord is gracious'.

Jeanie

(alt. Jeannie)

Shortened form of Jeanette, meaning 'the Lord is gracious'.

Jeanine

(alt. Jeannine)

Latin, meaning 'the Lord is gracious'.

Jemima

Hebrew, meaning 'dove'.

Jemma

Italian, meaning 'precious stone'.

Jena

Arabic, meaning 'little bird'.

Jenna

Hebrew, meaning 'the Lord is gracious'.

Jennifer

(alt. Jenifer)

Welsh, meaning 'white and smooth'.

Flower names

Acacia
Bluebell
Daisy
Flora
Hyacinth
Lilac
Petunia
Primrose
Rose
Snowdrop

J

267

Jenny
(alt. Jennie)
Shortened form of Jennifer, meaning 'white and smooth'.

Jerrie
(alt. Jeri, Jerri, Jerrie, Jerry)
German, meaning 'spear ruler'.

Jerusha
Hebrew, meaning 'married'.

Jeryl
English, meaning 'spear ruler'.

Jessa
Shortened form of Jessica, meaning 'He sees'.

Jessamy
(alt. Jessame, Jessamine, Jessamyn)
Persian, meaning 'jasmine flower'.

Jessica
(alt. Jesica, Jesika, Jessika)
Hebrew, meaning 'He sees'.

Jessie
(alt. Jesse, Jessi, Jessye)
Shortened form of Jessica, meaning 'He sees'.

Jesusa
Spanish, meaning 'mother of the Lord'.

Jethetha
Hebrew, meaning 'princess'.

Jette
(alt. Jetta, Jettie)
Danish, meaning 'black as coal'.

Jewel
(alt. Jewell)
French, meaning 'delight'.

Jezebel
(alt. Jezabel, Jezabelle)
Hebrew, meaning 'pure and virginal'. Now often used as a term for bad women.

Jill
Latin, meaning 'youthful'.

Jillian
Latin, meaning 'youthful'.

Jimena
Spanish, meaning 'heard'.

J

Jo

Shortened form of Joanna, meaning 'the Lord is gracious'.

Joan

Hebrew, meaning 'the Lord is gracious'.

Joanna

(alt. Joana, Joanie, Joann, Joanne, Johanna, Joni)

Hebrew, meaning 'the Lord is gracious'.

Jocasta

Italian, meaning 'lighthearted'.

Jocelyn

(alt. Jauslyn, Jocelyne, Joscelin, Joslyn)

German, meaning 'cheerful'.

Jody

(alt. Jodee, Jodi, Jodie)

Shortened form of Judith, meaning 'Jewish'.

Joelle

(alt. Joela)

Hebrew, meaning 'Jehovah is the Lord'.

Joie

French, meaning 'joy'.

Jolene

Contraction of Joanna and Darlene, meaning 'gracious darling'.

Jolie

(alt. Joely)

French, meaning 'pretty'.

Jordan

(alt. Jordana, Jordin, Jordyn)

Hebrew, meaning 'descend'.

Josephine

(alt. Josefina, Josephina)

Hebrew, meaning 'Jehovah increases'.

Josie

(alt. Joss, Jossie)

Shortened form of Josephine, meaning 'Jehovah increases'.

Jovita

(alt. Jovie)

Latin, meaning 'made glad'.

Joy

Latin, meaning 'joy'.

Joyce

Latin, meaning 'joyous'.

Juanita
(alt. Juana)
Spanish, meaning 'the Lord is gracious'.

Jubilee
Hebrew, meaning 'horn of a ram'.

Judith
(alt. Judit)
Hebrew, meaning 'Jewish'.

Judy
(alt. Judi, Judie)
Shortened form of Judith, Hebrew, meaning 'Jewish'.

Jules
French, meaning 'Jove's child'.

Julia
Latin, meaning 'youthful'.

Julianne
(alt. Juliana, Juliann, Julianne)
Latin, meaning 'youthful'

Julie
(alt. Juli)
Shortened form of Julia, meaning 'youthful'.

Juliet
(alt. Joliet, Juliette)
Latin, meaning 'youthful'. Most often associated with Shakespeare's heroine.

June
(alt. Juna)
Latin, after the month of the same name.

Juniper
Dutch, from the shrub of the same name.

Juno
(alt. Juneau)
Latin, meaning 'queen of heaven'.

Justice
English, meaning 'to deliver what is just'.

Justine
(alt. Justina)
Latin, meaning 'fair and righteous'.

Jørgina
Dutch, meaning 'farmer'.

 Girls' names

Kadenza
(alt. Kadence)
Latin, meaning 'with rhythm'.

Kadisha
Hebrew, meaning 'religious one'.

Kaitlin
(alt. Kaitlyn)
Greek, meaning 'pure'.

Kala
(alt. Kaela, Kaiala, Kaila)
Sanskrit, meaning 'black one'.

Kali
(alt. Kailee, Kailey, Kaleigh, Kaley, Kalie, Kalli, Kally, Kaylee, Kayleigh)
Sanskrit, meaning 'black one'.

Kalila
Arabic, meaning 'beloved'.

Kalina
Slavic, meaning 'flower'.

Kalliope
(alt. Calliope)
Greek, meaning 'beautiful voice'. From the muse of the same name.

Kallista
Greek, meaning 'most beautiful'.

Kama
Sanskrit, meaning 'love'.

Kami
Japanese, meaning 'lord'.

Place names

Adelaide
Atlanta
Brittany
Etna
Florence
India
Lydia
Madeira
Paris
Savannah

Kamilla
(alt. Kamilah)
Slavic, meaning 'serving girl'.

Kana
Hawaiian, from the demi-god of the same name.

Kandace
(alt. Kandice)
Latin, meaning 'glowing white'.

Kandy
(alt. Kandi)
Shortened form of Kandace, meaning 'glowing white'.

Kanika
African, meaning 'black cloth'.

Kara
Latin, meaning 'dear one'.

Karen
(alt. Karan, Karalyn, Karin, Karina, Karon, Karren)
Greek, meaning 'pure'.

Kari
(alt. Karie, Karri, Karrie)
Shortened form of Karen, meaning 'pure'.

Karimah
Arabic, meaning 'giving'.

Karishma
Sanskrit, meaning 'miracle'.

Karla
German, meaning 'man'.

Karly
(alt. Karlee, Karley, Karli)
German, meaning 'free man'.

Karlyn
German, meaning 'man'.

Karma
Hindi, meaning 'destiny'.

K

Karol
(alt. Karolina, Karolyn)
Slavic, meaning 'little and womanly'.

Kasey
(alt. Kacey, Kaci, Kacie, Kacy, Kasie, Kassie)
Irish Gaelic, meaning 'alert and watchful'.

Kassandra
Greek, meaning 'she who entangles men'.

Kasumi
Japanese, meaning 'of the mist'.

Katarina
(alt. Katarine, Katerina, Katharina)
Greek, meaning 'pure'.

Kate
(alt. Kat, Katie, Kathi, Kathie, Kathy, Kati, Katy)
Shortened form of Katherine, meaning 'pure'.

Katelyn
(alt. Katelin, Katelynn, Katlin, Katlyn)
Greek, meaning 'pure'.

Katherine
(alt. Katharine, Katheryn, Kathrine, Kathryn)
Greek, meaning 'pure'.

Kathleen
(alt. Kathlyn)
Greek, meaning 'pure'.

Katrina
(alt. Katina)
Greek, meaning 'pure'.

Kaveri
Indian, meaning 'sacred river'.

Kay
(alt. Kaye)
Shortened form of Katherine, meaning 'pure'.

Kayla
(alt. Kaylah)
Greek, meaning 'pure'.

Kayley
(alt. Kayley, Kayli)
American, meaning 'pure'.

Kaylin
American, meaning 'pure'.

K

Keeley
(alt. Keely)
Irish, meaning 'battle maid'.

Keila
Hebrew, meaning 'citadel'.

Keira
Irish Gaelic, meaning 'dark'.

Keisha
(alt. Keesha)
Arabic, meaning 'woman'.

Kelis
American, meaning 'beautiful'.

Kelly
(alt. Keli, Kelley, Kelli, Kellie)
Irish Gaelic, meaning 'battle maid'.

Kelsey
(alt. Kelcee, Kelcie, Kelsea, Kelsi, Kelsie)
English, meaning 'island'.

Kendall
(alt. Kendal)
English, meaning 'the valley of the River Kent'. Also a place in Cumbria.

Kendra
English, meaning 'knowing'.

Kenna
Irish Gaelic, meaning 'handsome'.

Kennedy
(alt. Kenadee, Kennedi)
Irish Gaelic, meaning 'helmet head'.

Kenya
African, from the country of the same name.

Kerensa
Cornish, meaning 'love'.

Kerrigan
Irish, meaning 'black haired'.

Kerry
(alt. Keri, Kerri, Kerrie)
Irish, from the county of the same name.

Khadijah
(alt. Khadejah)
Arabic, meaning 'premature baby'.

Kiana
(alt. Kia, Kiana)
American, meaning 'fibre'.

Kiara
Italian, meaning 'light'.

Kiki
Spanish, meaning 'home ruler'.

Kim
Shortened form of Kimberly, from the town of the same name.

Kimana
Native American, meaning 'butterfly'.

Kimberly
(alt. Kimberleigh, Kimberley)
Old English, meaning 'royal forest'.

Kingsley
(alt. Kinsley)
English, meaning 'king's meadow'.

Kinsey
English, meaning 'king's victory'.

Kira
Greek, meaning 'lady'.

Kiri
Maori, meaning 'tree bark'.

Long names

Alexandra
Benedicta
Christabelle
Constantine
Emmanuelle
Gabrielle
Henrietta
Philomena
Rosamond
Virginia

Kirsten
(alt. Kirstin)
Scandinavian, meaning 'Christian'.

Kirstie
(alt. Kirsty)
Shortened form of Kirsten, meaning 'Christian'.

Kitty
(alt. Kittie)
Shortened form of Katherine, meaning 'pure'.

Kizzy
Hebrew, meaning the plant 'cassia'.

K

Klara

Hungarian, meaning 'bright'.

Komal

Hindi, meaning 'soft and tender'.

Konstantina

Latin, meaning 'steadfast'.

Kora
(alt. Kori)

Greek, meaning 'maiden'.

Kris
(alt. Krista, Kristi, Kristie, Kristy)

Shortened form of Kristen, meaning 'Christian'.

Kristen
(alt. Kristan, Kristin, Kristine, Krysten)

Greek, meaning 'Christian'.

Krystal
(alt. Kristal, Kristel)

Greek, meaning 'ice'.

Kwanza
(alt. Kwanzaa)

African, meaning 'beginning'.

Kyla
(alt. Kya, Kylah, Kyle)

Scottish, meaning 'narrow spit of land'.

Kylie
(alt. Kiley, Kylee)

Irish Gaelic, meaning 'graceful'.

Kyoko

Japanese, meaning 'girl who sees her own true image'.

Kyra

Greek, meaning 'lady'.

Kyrie

Greek, meaning 'the Lord'.

Short names

Ali
Bev
Fay
Jan
Jo
Kay
Lyn
May
Nia
Val

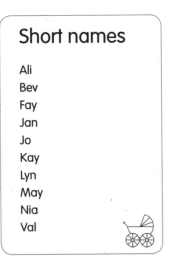

L Girls' names

Lacey
(alt. Laci, Lacie, Lacy)
French, from a nobleman's surname.

Ladonna
Italian, meaning 'lady'.

Lady
English, meaning 'bread kneader'.

Laidh
Hebrew, meaning 'lioness'.

Laila
(alt. Laelia, Layla, Leila, Lela, Lelah, Lelia)
Arabic, meaning 'night'.

Lainey
(alt. Laine, Laney)
French, meaning 'bright light'.

Lakeisha
(alt. Lakeshia)
American, meaning 'woman'.

Lakshmi
(alt. Laxmi)
Sanskrit, meaning 'good omen'. Also the Hindu goddess.

Lana
Greek, meaning 'light'.

Lani
(alt. Lanie)
Hawaiian, meaning 'sky'.

Lara
Latin, meaning 'famous'.

277

Laraine
French, meaning 'from Lorraine'.

Larissa
(alt. Larisa)
Greek, meaning 'lighthearted'.

Lark
(alt. Larkin)
English, meaning 'playful songbird'.

Larsen
Scandinavian, meaning 'son of Lars'.

Latifa
Arabic, meaning 'gentle and pleasant'.

Latika
(alt. Lotika)
Hindi, meaning 'a plant'.

Latisha
Latin, meaning 'happiness'.

Latona
(alt. Latonia)
Roman, from the mythological heroine of the same name.

Latoya
Spanish, meaning 'victorious one'.

Latrice
(alt. Latricia)
Latin, meaning 'noble'.

Laura
Latin, meaning 'laurel'.

Laurel
Latin, meaning 'laurel tree'.

Lauren
(alt. Lauran, Loren)
Latin, meaning 'laurel'.

Laveda
(alt. Lavada)
Latin, meaning 'cleansed'.

Lavender
Latin, from the plant of the same name.

Laverne
(alt. Lavern, Laverna)
Latin, from the goddess of the same name.

Lavinia
(alt. Lavina)

Latin, meaning 'woman of Rome'.

Lavita

American, meaning 'charming'.

Lavonne
(alt. Lavon)

French, meaning 'yew wood'.

Leah
(alt. Lea, Leia)

Hebrew, meaning 'weary'.

Leandra

Greek, meaning 'lion man'.

Leanne
(alt. Leann, Leanna, Leeann)

Contraction of Lee and Ann, meaning 'meadow grace'.

Leda

Greek, meaning 'gladness'.

Lee
(alt. Leigh)

English, meaning 'pasture or meadow'.

'Bad girl' names

Desdemona
Diva
Fifi
Lilith
Pandora
Peaches
Sadie
Scarlett
Tallulah
Xena

Leilani

Hawaiian, meaning 'flower from heaven'.

Leith

Scottish Gaelic, meaning 'broad river'.

Lena
(alt. Leena, Lina)

Latin, meaning 'light'.

Lenna
(alt. Lennie)

German, meaning 'lion's strength'.

Lenore
(alt. Lenora)

Greek, meaning 'light'.

L

Léonie

(alt. Leona, Leone)

Latin, meaning 'lion'.

Leonora

(alt. Leonor, Leonore)

Greek, meaning 'light'.

Leora

Greek, meaning 'light'.

Lerola

Latin, meaning 'like a blackbird'.

Leslie

(alt. Leslee, Lesley, Lesli)

Scottish Gaelic, meaning 'the grey castle'.

Leta

Latin, meaning 'glad and joyful'.

Letha

Greek, meaning 'forgetfulness'.

Letitia

(alt. Leticia, Lettice, Lettie)

Latin, meaning 'joy and gladness'.

Lexia

(alt. Lexie)

Greek, meaning 'defender of mankind'.

Lia

Italian, meaning 'bringer of the gospel'.

Liana

French, meaning 'to twine around'.

Libby

(alt. Libbie)

Shortened form of Elizabeth, meaning 'consecrated to God'.

Liberty

English, meaning 'freedom'.

Lida

Slavic, meaning 'loved by the people'.

Liese

(alt. Liesel, Liesl)

German, meaning 'pledged to God'.

Lila

(alt. Lilah)

Arabic, meaning 'night'.

Lilac

Latin, from the flower of the same name.

Lilia

(alt. Lilias)

Scottish, meaning 'lily'.

Lilith

Arabic, meaning 'ghost'.

Lillian

(alt. Lilian, Liliana, Lilla, Lillianna)

Latin, meaning 'lily'.

Lily

(alt. Lillie, Lilly)

Latin, from the flower of the same name.

Linda

(alt. Lynda)

Spanish, meaning 'pretty'.

Linden

(alt. Lindie, Lindy)

European, from the tree of the same name.

Lindsay

(alt. Lindsey, Linsey)

English, meaning 'island of linden trees'.

Linette

Welsh, meaning 'idol'.

Linnea

(alt. Linnae, Linny)

Scandinavian, meaning 'lime or linden tree'.

Liora

(alt. Lior)

Hebrew, meaning 'I have a light'.

Lirit

Hebrew, meaning 'musically talented'.

Lisa

(alt. Leesa, Lise, Liza)

Hebrew, meaning 'pledged to God'.

Lissa

Greek, meaning 'bee'.

Lissandra

(alt. Lisandra)

Greek, meaning 'man's defender'.

Liv

Nordic, meaning 'defence'.

Famous female singers

Adele (Adkins)
Annie (Lennox)
Billie (Holiday)
Dinah (Washington)
Ella (Fitzgerald)
Etta (James)
Florence (Welch)
Judy (Garland)
Kate (Bush)
Kylie (Minogue)
Lily (Allen)
Nina (Simone)

Livia
Latin, meaning 'olive'.

Liz
(alt. Lizzie, Lizzy)
Shortened form of Elizabeth, meaning 'consecrated to God'.

Logan
Irish Gaelic, meaning 'small hollow'.

Lois
German, meaning 'renowned in battle'.

Lola
Spanish, meaning 'sorrows'.

Lolita
Spanish, meaning 'sorrows'.

Lona
Latin, meaning 'lion'.

Lora
Latin, meaning 'laurel'.

Lorelei
(alt. Loralai, Loralie)
German, meaning 'dangerous rock'.

Lorenza
Latin, meaning 'from Laurentium'.

Loretta
(alt. Loreto)
Latin, meaning 'laurel'.

Lori
(alt. Laurie, Lorie, Lorri)
Latin, meaning 'laurel'.

Lorna
Scottish, from the town of Lorne.

Lorraine
(alt. Loraine)

French, meaning 'from Lorraine'.

Lottie
(alt. Lotta, Lotte)

French, meaning 'little and womanly'.

Lotus

Greek, meaning 'lotus flower'.

Lou
(alt. Louie, Lue)

Shortened form of Louise, meaning 'renowned in battle'.

Louise
(alt. Louisa, Luisa)

German, meaning 'renowned in battle'.

Lourdes

French, from the town of the same name.

Love

English, from the word 'love'.

Lowri

Welsh, meaning 'crowned with laurels'.

Luanne
(alt. Luann, Luanna)

German, meaning 'renowned in battle'.

Luba

Hebrew, meaning 'dearly loved'.

Lucia
(alt. Luciana)

Italian, meaning 'light'.

Lucille
(alt. Lucile, Lucilla)

French, meaning 'light'.

Lucinda

English, meaning 'light'.

Lucretia
(alt. Lucrece)

Spanish, meaning 'light'.

Lucy
(alt. Lucie)

Latin, meaning 'light'.

Ludmilla

Slavic, meaning 'beloved of the people'.

Luella

English, meaning 'renowned in battle'.

Lulu

(alt. Lula)

German, meaning 'renowned in battle'.

Luna

Latin, meaning 'moon'.

Lupita

Spanish, short form of Guadelupe. From the town of the same name.

Luz

Spanish, meaning 'light'.

Lydia

(alt. Lidia)

Greek, meaning 'from Lydia'.

Lynn

(alt. Lyn, Lynne)

Spanish, meaning 'pretty';
English, meaning 'waterfall'.

Lynton

English, meaning 'town of lime trees'.

Lyra

Latin, meaning 'lyre'.

Tennis players

Anna (Kournikova)
Billie Jean (King)
Justine (Henin)
Maria (Sharapova)
Monica (Seles)
Serena (Williams)
Sue (Barker)
Steffi (Graf)
Venus (Williams)

 Girls' names

Mab
Irish Gaelic, meaning 'joy'.

Mabel
(alt. Mabelle, Mable)
Latin, meaning 'loveable'.

Macaria
Spanish, meaning 'blessed'.

Machiko
Japanese, meaning 'beautiful woman'.

Macy
(alt. Macey, Maci, Macie)
French, meaning 'Matthew's estate'.

Mada
English, meaning 'from Magdala'.

Madden
(alt. Maddyn)
Irish, meaning 'little dog'.

Maddie
(alt. Maddi, Maddie, Madie)
Shortened form of Madeline, meaning 'from Magdala'.

Madeline
(alt. Madaline, Madalyn, Madeleine, Madelyn, Madelynn, Madilyn)
Greek, meaning 'from Magdala'.

Madge
Greek, meaning 'pearl'.

Madhuri
Hindi, meaning 'sweet girl'.

Madison
(alt. Maddison, Madisen, Madisyn, Madyson)
English, meaning 'son of the mighty warrior'.

Madonna
Latin, meaning 'my lady'.

Maeve
Irish Gaelic, meaning 'intoxicating'.

Mafalda
Spanish, meaning 'battle-mighty'.

Magali
Greek, meaning 'pearl'.

Magdalene
(alt. Magdalen, Magdalena)
Greek, meaning 'from Magdala'.

Maggie
Shortened form of Margaret, meaning 'pearl'.

Magnolia
Latin, from the flower of the same name.

Mahala
(alt. Mahalia)
Hebrew, meaning 'tender affection'.

Maia
(alt. Maja)
Greek, meaning 'mother'.

Maida
English, meaning 'maiden'.

Maisie
(alt. Maisey, Maisy, Maizie, Masie, Mazie)
Greek, meaning 'pearl'.

Madaio
Hawaiian, meaning 'gift from God'.

Malka
Hebrew, meaning 'queen'.

Mallory
(alt. Malorie)
French, meaning 'unhappy'.

Malvina
Gaelic, meaning 'smooth brow'.

Mamie
(alt. Mammie)
Shortened form of Margaret, meaning 'pearl'.

Mandy
(alt. Mandie)
Shortened form of Amanda, meaning 'much loved'.

Manisha
Sanskrit, meaning 'desire'.

Mansi
Hopi, meaning 'plucked flower'.

Manuela
Spanish, meaning 'the Lord is among us'.

Mara
Hebrew, meaning 'bitter'.

Marcela
(alt. Marceline, Marcella, Marcelle)
Latin, meaning 'war-like'.

Marcia
Latin, meaning 'war-like'.

Marcy
(alt. Marci, Marcie)
Latin, meaning 'war-like'.

Margaret
(alt. Margarete, Margaretta, Margarette, Margret)
Greek, meaning 'pearl'.

Margery
(alt. Marge, Margie, Margit, Margy)
French, meaning 'pearl'.

Margo
(alt. Margot)
French, meaning 'pearl'.

Marguerite
(alt. Margarita)
French, meaning 'pearl'.

Maria
(alt. Mariah)
Latin, meaning 'bitter'.

Marian
(alt. Mariam, Mariana, Marion)
French, meaning 'bitter grace'.

M

Marianne
(alt. Mariana, Mariann, Maryann, Maryanne)
French, meaning 'bitter grace'.

Maribel
American, meaning 'bitterly beautiful'.

Marie
French, meaning 'bitter'.

Mariel
(alt. Mariela, Mariella)
Dutch, meaning 'bitter'.

Marietta
(alt. Marieta)
French, meaning 'bitter'.

Marigold
English, from the flower of the same name.

Marika
Dutch, meaning 'bitter'.

Marilyn
(alt. Marilee, Marilene, Marilynn)
English, meaning 'bitter'.

Marin
American, from the county of the same name.

Marina
(alt. Marine)
Latin, meaning 'from the sea'.

Mariposa
Spanish, meaning 'butterfly'.

Maris
Latin, meaning 'of the sea'.

Marisa
Latin, meaning 'of the sea'.

Marisol
Spanish, meaning 'bitter sun'.

Marissa
American, meaning 'of the sea'.

Marjolaine
French, meaning 'marjoram'.

Marjorie
(alt. Marjory)
French, meaning 'pearl'.

Marla
Shortened form of Marlene, meaning 'bitter'.

Marlene
(alt. Marlen, Marlena)
Hebrew, meaning 'bitter'.

Marley
(alt. Marlee)
American, meaning 'bitter'.

Marlo
(alt. Marlowe)
American, meaning 'bitter'.

Marseille
French, from the city of the same name.

Marsha
English, meaning 'war-like'.

Martha
(alt. Marta)
Aramaic, meaning 'lady'.

Martina
Latin, meaning 'war-like'.

Marvel
French, meaning 'something to marvel at'.

Mary
Hebrew, meaning 'bitter'.

Masada
Hebrew, meaning 'foundation'.

Matilda
(alt. Mathilda, Mathilde, Matide)
German, meaning 'battle-mighty'.

Mattea
Hebrew, meaning 'gift of God'.

Maude
(alt. Maud)
German, meaning 'battle-mighty'.

Maura
Irish, meaning 'bitter'.

Maureen
(alt. Maurine)
Irish, meaning 'bitter'.

Mavis
French, meaning 'thrush'.

Maxine
(alt. Maxie)
Latin, meaning 'greatest'.

M

May
(alt. Mae, Maya, Maye, Mayra)
Hebrew, meaning 'gift of God'.
Also the month.

Mckenna
(alt. Mackenna)
Irish Gaelic, meaning 'son of the handsome one'.

Mckenzie
(alt. Mackenzie, Mckenzy, Mikenzi)
Irish Gaelic, meaning 'son of the wise ruler'.

Meara
Gaelic, meaning 'filled with happiness'.

Medea
(alt. Meda)
Greek, meaning 'ruling'.

Meg
Shortened form of Margaret, meaning 'pearl'.

Megan
(alt. Meagan, Meghan)
Welsh, meaning 'pearl'.

Mehitabel
Hebrew, meaning 'benefited by God'.

Mehri
Persian, meaning 'kind'.

Meiwei
Chinese, meaning 'forever enchanting'.

Melanie
(alt. Melania, Melany, Melonie)
Greek, meaning 'dark-skinned'.

Melba
Australian, meaning 'from Melbourne'.

Melia
(alt. Meliah)
German, meaning 'industrious'.

Melina
Greek, meaning 'honey'.

Melinda
Latin, meaning 'honey'.

Melisande
French, meaning 'bee'.

Melissa
(alt. Melisa, Mellissa)
Greek, meaning 'bee'.

Melody
(alt. Melodie)
Greek, meaning 'song'.

Melvina
Celtic, meaning 'chieftain'.

Menora
Hebrew, meaning 'candlestick'.

Mercedes
Spanish, meaning 'mercies'.
Most often associated with the
car.

Mercy
English, meaning 'mercy'.

Meredith
(alt. Meridith)
Welsh, meaning 'great ruler'.

Merle
French, meaning 'blackbird'.

Merry
English, meaning 'lighthearted'.

Meryl
(alt. Merrill)
Irish Gaelic, meaning 'sea-bright'.

Meta
German, meaning 'pearl'.

Mia
Italian, meaning 'mine'.

Michaela
(alt. Makaela, Makaila, Micaela, Mikaila, Mikayla)
Hebrew, meaning 'who is like the Lord'.

Michelle
(alt. Machelle, Mechelle, Michaele, Michal, Michele)
French, meaning 'who is like the Lord'.

Mickey
(alt. Mickie)
Shortened form of Michelle, meaning 'who is like the Lord'.

Mieko
Japanese, meaning 'born into wealth'.

Migdalia
Greek, meaning 'from Magdala'.

Mignon
French, meaning 'cute'.

M

Mika
(alt. Micah)
Hebrew, meaning 'who resembles God'.

Milada
Czech, meaning 'my love'.

Milagros
Spanish, meaning 'miracles'.

Milan
Italian, from the city of the same name.

Mildred
English, meaning 'gentle strength'.

Milena
Czech, meaning 'love and warmth'.

Miley
American, meaning 'smiley'. Made popular by Miley Cyrus.

Millicent
German, meaning 'high-born power'.

Millie
(alt. Milly)
Shortened form of Millicent, meaning 'high-born power'.

Mimi
Italian, meaning 'bitter'.

Popular song names

Alice (*All the Girls Love Alice*, Elton John)
Billie Jean (*Billie Jean*, Michael Jackson)
Caroline (*Sweet Caroline*, Neil Diamond)
Delilah (*Delilah*, Tom Jones)
Eileen (*Come on Eileen*, Dexy's Midnight Runners)
Eleanor (*Eleanor Rigby*, The Beatles)
Judy (*Judy*, The Beach Boys)
Roxanne (*Roxanne*, The Police)
Sally (*Mustang Sally*, Wilson Pickett)
Valerie (*Valerie*, Amy Winehouse & Mark Ronson)

Mina
(alt. Mena)

German, meaning 'love'.

Mindy
(alt. Mindi)

Latin, meaning 'honey'.

Minerva

Roman, from the goddess of the same name.

Ming

Chinese, meaning 'bright'.

Minna

German, meaning 'helmet'.

Minnie

German, meaning 'helmet'. Often associated with the Disney character Minnie Mouse.

Mira

Latin, meaning 'admirable'.

Mirabel
(alt. Mirabella, Mirabelle)

Latin, meaning 'wonderful'.

Miranda
(alt. Meranda)

Latin, meaning 'admirable'.

Mirella
(alt. Mireille, Mirela)

Latin, meaning 'admirable'.

Miriam

Hebrew, meaning 'bitter'.

Mirta

Spanish, meaning 'crown of thorns'.

Missy

Shortened form of Melissa, meaning 'bee'.

Misty
(alt. Misti)

English, meaning 'mist'.

Mitzi

German, meaning 'bitter'.

Miu

Japanese, meaning 'beautiful feather'.

Moira
(alt. Maira)

Irish, meaning 'bitter'.

M

Molly
(alt. Mollie)

American, meaning 'bitter'.

Mona

Irish Gaelic, meaning 'aristocratic'.

Monica
(alt. Monika, Monique)

Latin, meaning 'adviser'.

Montserrat
(alt. Monserrate)

Spanish, from the town of the same name.

Morag

Scottish, meaning 'star of the sea'.

Morgan
(alt. Morgann)

Welsh, meaning 'great and bright'.

Moriah

Hebrew, meaning 'the Lord is my teacher'.

Morwenna

Welsh, meaning 'maiden'.

Moselle
(alt. Mozell, Mozella, Mozelle)

Hebrew, meaning 'saviour'.

Mulan

Chinese, meaning 'wood orchid'.

Munin

Scandinavian, meaning 'good memory'.

Muriel

Irish Gaelic, meaning 'sea-bright'.

Mya
(alt. Myah)

Greek, meaning 'mother'.

Myfanwy

Welsh, meaning 'my little lovely one'.

Myra

Latin, meaning 'scented oil'.

Myrna
(alt. Mirna)

Irish Gaelic, meaning 'tender and beloved'.

Myrtle

Irish, from the shrub of the same name.

M

 Girls' names

Nadia
(alt. Nadya)
Russian, meaning 'hope'.

Nadine
French, meaning 'hope'.

Nahara
Aramaic, meaning 'light'.

Naima
Arabic, meaning 'water nymph'.

Nakia
Egyptian, meaning 'pure'.

Nalani
Hawaiian, meaning 'serenity of the skies'.

Nan
(alt. Nanna, Nannie)
Hebrew, meaning 'grace'.

Nancy
(alt. Nanci, Nancie)
Hebrew, meaning 'grace'.

Nanette
(alt. Nannette)
French, meaning 'grace'.

Naomi
(alt. Naoma, Noemi)
Hebrew, meaning 'pleasant'.

Narcissa
Greek, meaning 'daffodil'.

Nastasia

Greek, meaning 'resurrection'.

Natalie

(alt. Natalee, Natalia, Natalya, Nathalie)

Latin, meaning 'birth day'.

Natasha

(alt. Natasa)

Russian, meaning 'birth day'.

Natividad

Spanish, meaning 'Christmas'.

Neda

English, meaning 'wealthy'.

Nedra

English, meaning 'underground'.

Neema

Swahili, meaning 'born of prosperity'.

Neka

Native American, meaning 'goose'.

Nell

(alt. Nelda, Nell, Nella, Nellie, Nelly)

Shortened form of Eleanor, meaning 'light'.

Nemi

Italian, from the lake of the same name.

Neoma

Greek, meaning 'new moon'.

Nereida

Spanish, meaning 'sea nymph'.

Nerissa

Greek, meaning 'sea nymph'.

Nettie

(alt. Neta)

Shortened form of Henrietta, meaning 'ruler of the house'.

Neva

Spanish, meaning 'snowy'.

Nevaeh

American, meaning 'heaven'.

Nhung

Vietnamese, meaning 'velvet'.

Niamh
(alt. Neve)
Irish, meaning 'brightness'.

Nicki
(alt. Nicky, Nikki)
Shortened form of Nicola, meaning 'victory of the people'.

Nicola
Greek, meaning 'victory of the people'.

Nicole
(alt. Nichol, Nichole, Nicolette, Nicolle, Nikole)
Greek, meaning 'victory of the people'.

Nidia
Spanish, meaning 'graceful'.

Nigella
Irish Gaelic, meaning 'champion'.

Nikita
Greek, meaning 'unconquered'.

Nila
Egyptian, meaning 'Nile'.

Nilda
German, meaning 'battle woman'.

Nimra
Arabic, meaning 'number'.

Nina
Spanish, meaning 'girl'.

Nissa
Hebrew, meaning 'sign'.

Nita
Spanish, meaning 'gracious'.

Nixie
German, meaning 'water sprite'.

Noel
(alt. Noelle)
French, meaning 'Christmas'.

Nola
Irish Gaelic, meaning 'white shoulder'.

Nona
Latin, meaning 'ninth'.

N

Nora
(alt. Norah)
Shortened form of Eleanor, meaning 'light'.

Noreen
(alt. Norine)
Irish, meaning 'light'.

Norma
Latin, meaning 'pattern'.

Normandie
(alt. Normandy)
French, from the province of the same name.

Novia
Latin, meaning 'new'.

Nuala
Irish Gaelic, meaning 'white shoulder'.

Nydia
Latin, meaning 'nest'.

Nyimbo
Swahili, meaning 'song'.

Nysa
(alt. Nyssa)
Greek, meaning 'ambition'.

Names of goddesses

Aphrodite (Love: Greek)
Ceres (Agriculture: Roman)
Eos (Dawn: Greek)
Hestia (Hearth: Greek)
Kali (Death: Indian)
Lucinda (Childbirth: Roman)
Minerva (Wisdom: Roman)
Nephthys (Death: Egyptian)
Sesheta (Stars: Egyptian)
Terra (Earth: Roman)

N

Girls' names

Oceana
(alt. Ocean, Océane, Ocie)
Greek, meaning 'ocean'.

Octavia
Latin, meaning 'eighth'.

Oda
(alt. Odie)
Shortened form of Odessa, meaning 'long voyage'.

Odele
(alt. Odell)
English, meaning 'woad hill'.

Odelia
Hebrew, meaning 'I will praise the Lord'.

Odessa
Greek, meaning 'long voyage'.

Odette
(alt. Odetta)
French, meaning 'wealthy'.

Odile
(alt. Odilia)
French, meaning 'prospers in battle'.

Odina
Feminine form of Odin, from the Nordic god of the same name, meaning 'creative inspiration'.

Odyssey
Greek, meaning 'long journey'.

O

Oksana
Russian, meaning 'praise to God'.

Ola
(alt. Olie)
Greek, meaning 'man's defender'.

Olena
(alt. Olene)
Russian, meaning 'light'.

Olga
Russian, meaning 'holy'.

Oliana
American, meaning 'the Lord has answered'.

Olivia
(alt. Olivev, Oliviana, Olivié)
Latin, meaning 'olive'. The UK's most popular girls' name in 2011.

Ollie
Shortened form of Olivia, meaning 'olive'.

Olwen
Welsh, meaning 'white footprint'.

Olympia
(alt. Olimpia)
Greek, meaning 'from Mount Olympus'.

Oma
(alt. Omie)
Arabic, meaning 'leader'.

Omyra
Latin, meaning 'scented oil'.

Ona
(alt. Onnie)
Shortened form of Oneida, meaning 'long awaited'.

Ondine
French, meaning 'wave of water'.

Oneida
Native American, meaning 'long awaited'.

Onyx
Latin, meaning 'veined gem'.

Oona
Irish, meaning 'unity'.

O

Opal

Sanskrit, meaning 'gem'.

Ophelia

(alt. Ofelia, Ophélie)

Greek, meaning 'help'. Best known from Shakespeare's play *Hamlet*.

Oprah

Hebrew, meaning 'young deer'. Most often associated with Oprah Winfrey.

Ora

Latin, meaning 'prayer'.

Orabela

Latin, meaning 'prayer'.

Oralie

(alt. Oralia)

French, meaning 'golden'.

Orane

French, meaning 'rising'.

Orchid

Greek, from the flower of the same name.

Oriana

(alt. Oriane)

Latin, meaning 'dawning'.

Orla

(alt. Orlaith, Orly)

Irish Gaelic, meaning 'golden lady'.

Orlean

French, meaning 'plum'.

Ornelia

Italian, meaning 'flowering ash tree'.

Orsa

(alt. Osia, Ossie)

Latin, meaning 'bear'.

Colour names

Azure
Cinnabar
Ebony
Fuchsia
Ivory
Olive
Rose
Saffron
Sienna
Violet

Otthid

Greek, meaning 'prospers in battle'.

Ottilie
(alt. Ottie)

French, meaning 'prospers in battle'.

Ouida

French, meaning 'renowned in battle'.

Oyintsa

Native American, meaning 'white duck'.

Ozette

Native American, from the village of the same name.

Popular North American names

Abigail	Isabella
Ava	Madison
Chloe	Mia
Emily	Olivia
Emma	Sophia

O

Girls' names

Pacifica
(alt. Pacifika)
Spanish, meaning 'peaceful'.

Padma
Sanskrit, meaning 'lotus'.

Paige
(alt. Page)
French, meaning 'serving boy'.

Paisley
Scottish, from the town of the same name.

Palma
(alt. Palmira)
Latin, meaning 'palm tree'.

Paloma
Spanish, meaning 'dove'.

Pam
Shortened form of Pamela, meaning 'all honey'.

Pamela
(alt. Pamala, Pamella, Pamla)
Greek, meaning 'all honey'.

Pandora
Greek, meaning 'all gifted'. Also from the Greek myth.

Pangiota
Greek, meaning 'all is holy'.

Paniz
Persian, meaning 'candy'.

Pansy
French, from the flower of the same name.

303

Paprika
English, meaning 'spice'.

Paradisa
(alt. Paradis)
Greek, meaning 'garden orchard'.

Paris
(alt. Parisa)
Greek, from the mythological hero of the same name. Also from the city.

Parker
English, meaning 'park keeper'.

Parthenia
Greek, meaning 'virginal'.

Parthenope
Greek, from the mythological Siren of the same name.

Parvati
Sanskrit, meaning 'daughter of the mountain'.

Pascale
French, meaning 'Easter'.

Pat
(alt. Patsy, Patti, Pattie, Patty)
Shortened form of Patricia, meaning 'noble'.

Patience
French, meaning 'the state of being patient'.

Patricia
(alt. Patrice)
Latin, meaning 'noble'.

Paula
Latin, meaning 'small'.

Pauline
(alt. Paulette, Paulina)
Latin, meaning 'small'.

Paxton
Latin, meaning 'peaceful town'.

Paz
Spanish, meaning 'peace'.

Pazia
Hebrew, meaning 'golden'.

Peace
English, meaning 'peace'.

Gem and precious stone names

Amber
Beryl
Coral
Esmerelda
Jade
Marjorie
Pearl
Ruby
Topaz

Peaches

English, meaning 'peaches'.

Pearl
(alt. Pearle, Pearlie, Perla)

Latin, meaning 'pale gemstone'.

Peggy
(alt. Peggie)

Greek, meaning 'pearl'.

Pelia

Hebrew, meaning 'marvel of God'.

Penelope

Greek, meaning 'bobbin worker'.

Penny
(alt. Penni, Pennie)

Greek, meaning 'bobbin worker'.

Peony

Greek, from the flower of the same name.

Perdita

Latin, meaning 'lost'.

Peri
(alt. Perri)

Hebrew, meaning 'outcome'.

Perry

French, meaning 'pear tree'.

Persephone

Greek, meaning 'bringer of destruction'.

Petra
(alt. Petrina)

Greek, meaning 'rock'.

Petula

Latin, meaning 'to seek'.

P

Petunia
Greek, from the flower of the same name.

Phaedra
Greek, meaning 'bright'.

Philippa
Greek, meaning 'horse lover'.

Philomena
(alt. Philoma)
Greek, meaning 'loved one'.

Phoebe
Greek, meaning 'shining and brilliant'.

Phoenix
Greek, meaning 'red as blood'. Also from the mythical bird.

Phyllida
Greek, meaning 'leafy bough'.

Phyllis
(alt. Phillia, Phylis)
Greek, meaning 'leafy bough'.

Pia
Latin, meaning 'pious'.

Piera
Italian, meaning 'rock'.

Pilar
Spanish, meaning 'pillar'.

Piper
English, meaning 'pipe player'.

Pippa
Shortened form of Philippa, meaning 'horse lover'.

Popular Asian names

Amaya	Kai
Aoi	Miya
Hana	Murasaki
Hiro	Niu
Iku	Rei

P

Plum

Latin, from the fruit of the same name.

Polly

Hebrew, meaning 'bitter'.

Pomona

Latin, meaning 'apple'.

Poppy

Latin, from the flower of the same name.

Portia

(alt. Porsha)

Latin, meaning 'from the Portia clan'.

Posy

English, meaning 'small flower'.

Precious

Latin, meaning 'of great worth'.

Priela

Hebrew, meaning 'fruit of God'.

Primavera

Spanish, meaning 'springtime'.

Primrose

English, meaning 'first rose'.

Princess

English, meaning 'daughter of the monarch'.

Priscilla

(alt. Prisca, Priscila)

Latin, meaning 'ancient'.

Priya

Hindi, meaning 'loved one'.

Prudence

Latin, meaning 'caution'.

Prudie

Shortened form of Prudence, meaning 'caution'.

Prunella

Latin, meaning 'small plum'.

Psyche

Greek, meaning 'breath'. Also from Greek mythology and psychological theory.

Names with positive meanings

Allegra – cheerful
Augusta – magnificent
Felicia – lucky
Gladys – glad
Hilary – cheerful

Lucy – light
Phoebe – radiant
Rinah – joyful
Thalia – flourishing
Yoko – positive

 Girls' names

Qiana
(alt. Qianah, Qiania, Qyana, Qianne)

American, meaning 'gracious'.

Qiturah
Arabic, meaning 'incense'.

Queen
(alt. Queenie)
English, meaning 'queen'.

Quiana
American, meaning 'silky'.

Quincy
(alt. Quincey)
French, meaning 'estate of the fifth son'.

Quinn
Irish Gaelic, meaning 'counsel'.

Quintessa
Latin, meaning 'creative'.

Foreign alternatives

Emily – Emilie, Emeline
Helen – Galina, Helene
Mary – Marie, Maria, Marjan
Sarah – Sara, Sarine, Zara
Violet – Iolanthe, Yolanda

Q

Palindrome names

Aja	Ette
Anna	Eve
Anona	Hannah
Elle	Ono
Emme	Viv

R Girls' names

Rachel
(alt. Rachael, Rachelle)
Hebrew, meaning 'ewe'.

Radhika
Sanskrit, meaning 'prosperous'.

Rae
(alt. Ray)
Shortened form of Rachel, meaning 'ewe'.

Rafferty
Irish, meaning 'abundance'.

Rahima
Arabic, meaning 'compassionate'.

Raina
(alt. Rain, Raine, Rainey, Rayne)
Latin, meaning 'queen'.

Raissa
(alt. Raisa)
Yiddish, meaning 'rose'.

Raleigh
(alt. Rayleigh)
English, meaning 'meadow of roe deer'.

Rama
(alt. Ramey, Ramya)
Hebrew, meaning 'exalted'.

Ramona
(alt. Romona)
Spanish, meaning 'wise guardian'.

Ramsey
English, meaning 'raven island'.

Rana
(alt. Rania, Rayna)

Arabic, meaning 'beautiful thing'.

Randy
(alt. Randi)

Shortened form of Miranda, meaning 'admirable'.

Rani
Sanskrit, meaning 'queen'.

Raphaela
(alt. Rafaela, Raffaella)

Spanish, meaning 'healing God'.

Raquel
(alt. Racquel)

Hebrew, meaning 'ewe'.

Rashida
Turkish, meaning 'righteous'.

Raven
(alt. Ravyn)

English, from the bird of the same name.

Razia
Arabic, meaning 'contented'.

Reagan
(alt. Reagen, Regan)

Irish Gaelic, meaning 'descendant of Riagán'.

Reba
Shortened form of Rebecca, meaning 'joined'.

Rebecca
(alt. Rebekah)

Hebrew, meaning 'joined'.

Reese
Welsh, meaning 'fiery and zealous'.

Regina
Latin, meaning 'queen'.

Reiko
Japanese, meaning 'thankful one'.

Reina
(alt. Reyna, Rheyna)

Spanish, meaning 'queen'.

Rena
(alt. Reena)

Hebrew, meaning 'serene'.

Renata
Latin, meaning 'reborn'.

Rene
Greek, meaning 'peace'.

Renée
(alt. Renae)
French, meaning 'reborn'.

Renita
Latin, meaning 'resistant'.

Reshma
(alt. Resha)
Sanskrit, meaning 'silk'.

Reta
(alt. Retha, Retta)
Shortened form of Margaret, meaning 'pearl'.

Rhea
Greek, meaning 'earth'.

Rheta
Greek, meaning 'eloquent speaker'.

Rhiannon
(alt. Reanna, Reanne, Rhian, Rhianna)
Welsh, meaning 'witch'.

Rhoda
Greek, meaning 'rose'.

Rhona
Nordic, meaning 'rough island'.

Rhonda
(alt. Ronda)
Welsh, meaning 'noisy'.

Ría
(alt. Rie, Riya)
Shortened form of Victoria, meaning 'victor'.

Ricki
(alt. Rieko, Rika, Rikki)
Shortened form of Frederica, meaning 'peaceful ruler'.

Riley
Irish Gaelic, meaning 'courageous'.

Rilla
German, meaning 'small brook'.

Rima
Arabic, meaning 'antelope'.

Riona

Irish Gaelic, meaning 'like a queen'.

Ripley

English, meaning 'shouting man's meadow'.

Risa

Latin, meaning 'laughter'.

Rita

Shortened form of Margaret, meaning 'pearl'.

River

(alt. Riviera)

English, from the body of water of the same name.

Robbie

(alt. Robi, Roby)

Shortened form of Roberta, meaning 'bright fame'.

Roberta

English, meaning 'bright fame'.

Robin

(alt. Robbin, Robyn)

English, meaning 'bright fame'.

Rochelle

(alt. Richelle, Rochel)

French, meaning 'little rock'.

Rogue

French, meaning 'beggar'.

Rohina

(alt. Rohini)

Sanskrit, meaning 'sandalwood'.

Roja

Spanish, meaning 'red-haired lady'.

Roisin

Irish Gaelic, meaning 'little rose'.

Rolanda

German, meaning 'famous land'.

Roma

Italian, meaning 'Rome'.

Romaine

(alt. Romina)

French, meaning 'from Rome'.

'Powerful' names

Adira
Edrea
Isis
Ricarda
Roxie
Ulrika

Romola
(alt. Romilda, Romily)

Latin, meaning 'Roman woman'.

Romy

Shortened form of Rosemary, meaning 'dew of the sea'.

Rona
(alt. Ronia, Ronja, Ronna)

Nordic, meaning 'rough island'.

Ronnie
(alt. Roni)

English, meaning 'strong counsel'.

Roro

Indonesian, meaning 'nobility'.

Rosa

Italian, meaning 'rose'.

Rosabel
(alt. Rosabella)

Contraction of Rose and Belle, meaning 'beautiful rose'.

Rosalie
(alt. Rosale, Rosalia, Rosalina)

French, meaning 'rose garden'.

Rosalind
(alt. Rosalinda)

Spanish, meaning 'pretty rose'.

Rosalyn
(alt. Rosaleen, Rosaline, Roselyn)

Contraction of Rose and Lynn, meaning 'pretty rose'.

Rosamond
(alt. Rosamund)

German, meaning 'renowned protector'.

Rose

Latin, from the flower of the same name.

R

Roseanne
(alt. Rosana, Rosann, Rosanna, Rosanne, Roseann, Roseanna)

Contraction of Rose and Anne, meaning 'graceful rose'.

Rosemary
(alt. Rosemarie)

Latin, meaning 'dew of the sea'.

Rosie
(alt. Rosia)

Shortened form of Rosemary, meaning 'dew of the sea'.

Rosita

Spanish, meaning 'rose'.

Rowena
(alt. Rowan)

Welsh, meaning 'slender and fair'.

Roxanne
(alt. Roxana, Roxane, Roxanna)

Persian, meaning 'dawn'.

Roxie

Shortened form of Roxanne, meaning 'dawn'.

Rubena
(alt. Rubina)

Hebrew, meaning 'behold, a son'.

Ruby
(alt. Rubi, Rubie)

English, meaning 'red gemstone'.

Rusty

American, meaning 'red-headed'.

Ruth
(alt. Ruthe, Ruthie)

Hebrew, meaning 'friend and companion'.

Popular Irish names

Aoife
Bree
Caitlin
Ciara
Eilis
Molly
Niamh
Orlaith
Shannon
Sinead

R

 Girls' names

Saba
(alt. Sabah)
Greek, meaning 'from Sheba'.

Sabina
(alt. Sabine)
Latin, meaning 'from the Sabine tribe'.

Sabrina
Latin, meaning 'the River Severn'.

Sadella
American, meaning 'fairytale princess'.

Sadie
(alt. Sade, Sadye)
Hebrew, meaning 'princess'.

Saffron
English, from the spice of the same name.

Safiya
Arabic, meaning 'sincere friend'.

Sage
(alt. Saga, Saige)
Latin, meaning 'wise and healthy'.

Sahara
Arabic, meaning 'desert'.

Sakura
Japanese, meaning 'cherry blossom'.

Sally
(alt. Sallie)
Hebrew, meaning 'princess'.

Salome
(alt. Salma)
Hebrew, meaning 'peace'.

Sam
(alt. Sammie, Sammy)
Shortened form of Samantha, meaning 'told by God'.

Samantha
Hebrew, meaning 'told by God'.

Samara
(alt. Samaria, Samira)
Hebrew, meaning 'under God's rule'.

Sanaa
Arabic, meaning 'brilliance'.

Sandra
(alt. Saundra)
Shortened form of Alexandra, meaning 'defender of mankind'.

Sandy
(alt. Sandi)
Shortened form of Sandra, meaning 'defender of mankind'.

Sangeeta
Hindi, meaning 'musical'.

Sanna
(alt. Saniya, Sanne, Sanni)
Hebrew, meaning 'lily'.

Santana
(alt. Santina)
Spanish, meaning 'holy'.

Saoirse
Irish, meaning 'freedom'.

Sapphire
(alt. Saphira)
Hebrew, meaning 'blue gemstone'.

Sarah
(alt. Sara, Sarai, Sariah)
Hebrew, meaning 'princess'.

Sasha
(alt. Sacha, Sascha)
Russian, meaning 'man's defender'.

S

Saskia
(alt. Saskie)
Dutch, meaning 'the Saxon people'.

Savannah
(alt. Savanah, Savanna, Savina)
Spanish, meaning 'treeless'.

Scarlett
(alt. Scarlet)
English, meaning 'scarlet'.

Scout
French, meaning 'to listen'.

Sedona
(alt. Sedna)
Spanish, from the city of the same name.

Selah
(alt Sela)
Hebrew, meaning 'cliff'.

Selby
English, meaning 'manor village'.

Selena
(alt. Salena, Salima, Salina, Selene, Selina)
Greek, meaning 'moon goddess'.

Selma
German, meaning 'Godly helmet'.

Seneca
Native American, meaning 'from the Seneca tribe'.

Sephora
Hebrew, meaning 'bird'.

September
Latin, meaning 'seventh month'.

Seraphina
(alt. Serafina, Seraphia, Seraphine)
Hebrew, meaning 'ardent'.

Serena
(alt. Sarina, Sereana)
Latin, meaning 'tranquil'.

Serenity
Latin, meaning 'serene'.

Shania
(alt. Shaina, Shana, Shaniya)
Hebrew, meaning 'beautiful'.

Shanice

American, meaning 'from Africa'.

Shaniqua

(alt. Shanika)

African, meaning 'warrior princess'.

Shanna

English, meaning 'old'.

Shannon

(alt. Shannan, Shanon)

Irish Gaelic, meaning 'old and ancient'.

Shantal

(alt. Shantel, Shantell)

French, meaning 'stone'.

Shanti

Hindi, meaning 'peaceful'.

Sharlene

German, meaning 'man'.

Sharon

(alt. Sharen, Sharona, Sharron, Sharyn)

Hebrew, meaning 'a plain'.

Nautical names

Coral
Halimedi
Marina
Nereida
Sagara

Shasta

American, from the mountain of the same name.

Shauna

(alt. Shawna)

Irish, meaning 'the Lord is gracious'.

Shayla

(alt. Shaylie, Shayna, Sheyla)

Irish, meaning 'blind'.

Shea

Irish Gaelic, meaning 'from the fairy fort'.

Sheena

Irish, meaning 'the Lord is gracious'.

S

Sheila
(alt. Shelia)
Irish, meaning 'blind'.

Shelby
(alt. Shelba, Shelbie)
English, meaning 'estate on the ledge'.

Shelley
(alt. Shelli, Shellie, Shelly)
English, meaning 'meadow on the ledge'.

Shenandoah
Native American, meaning 'after an Oneida chief'.

Sheridan
Irish Gaelic, meaning 'wild man'.

Sherry
(alt. Sheree, Sheri, Sherie, Sherri, Sherrie)
Shortened form of Cheryl, meaning 'man'.

Sheryl
(alt. Sherryl)
German, meaning 'man'.

Shiloh
Hebrew, meaning 'his gift'. From the biblical place of the same name.

Shirley
(alt. Shirlee)
English, meaning 'bright meadow'.

Shivani
Sanskrit, meaning 'wife of Shiva'.

Shona
Irish Gaelic, meaning 'God is gracious'.

Shoshana
(alt. Shoshanna)
Hebrew, meaning 'lily'.

Shura
Russian, meaning 'man's defender'.

Sian
(alt. Sianna)
Welsh, meaning 'the Lord is gracious'.

Sibyl
(alt. Sybil)
Greek, meaning 'seer and oracle'.

Sidney
(alt. Sydney)
English, meaning 'from St Denis'.

Sidonie
(alt. Sidonia, Sidony)
Latin, meaning 'from Sidonia'.

Siena
(alt. Sienna)
Latin, from the town of the same name.

Sierra
Spanish, meaning 'saw'.

Siffhi
Hindi, meaning 'spiritual powers'.

Signa
(alt. Signe)
Scandinavian, meaning 'victory'.

Sigrid
Nordic, meaning 'fair victory'.

Silja
Scandinavian, meaning 'blind'.

Simcha
Hebrew, meaning 'joy'.

Simone
(alt. Simona)
Hebrew, meaning 'listening intently'.

Sinead
Irish, meaning 'the Lord is gracious'.

Siobhan
Irish, meaning 'the Lord is gracious'.

Siren
(alt. Sirena)
Greek, meaning 'entangler'.

Siria
Spanish, meaning 'glowing'.

Sisika
Native American, meaning 'like a bird'.

S

Skye
(alt. Sky)
Scottish, from the island of the same name.

Skyler
(alt. Skyla, Skylar)
Dutch, meaning 'giving shelter'.

Sloane
(alt. Sloan)
Irish Gaelic, meaning 'man of arms'.

Socorro
Spanish, meaning 'to aid'.

Sojourner
English, meaning 'temporary stay'.

Solana
Spanish, meaning 'sunlight'.

Solange
French, meaning 'with dignity'.

Soledad
Spanish, meaning 'solitude'.

Soleil
French, meaning 'sun'.

Solveig
Scandinavian, meaning 'woman of the house'.

Sona
Arabic, meaning 'golden one'.

Sonia
(alt. Sonja, Sonya)
Greek, meaning 'wisdom'.

Sophia
(alt. Sofia, Sofie, Sophie)
Greek, meaning 'wisdom'.

Sophronia
Greek, meaning 'sensible'.

Soraya
Persian, meaning 'princess'.

Sorcha
Irish Gaelic, meaning 'bright and shining'.

Sorrel
English, from the herb of the same name.

Stacey
(alt. Stacie, Stacy)
Greek, meaning 'resurrection'.

S

Star
(alt. Starla, Starr)
English, meaning 'star'.

Stella
Latin, meaning 'star'.

Stephanie
(alt. Stefanie, Stephani, Stephania, Stephany)
Greek, meaning 'crowned'.

Sue
(alt. Susie, Suzy)
Shortened form of Susan, meaning 'lily'.

Sukey
(alt. Sukey, Sukie)
Shortened form of Susan, meaning 'lily'.

Summer
English, from the season of the same name.

Sunday
English, meaning 'the first day'.

Sunny
(alt. Sun)
English, meaning 'of a pleasant temperament'.

Suri
Persian, meaning 'red rose'.

Surya
Hindi, from the god of the same name.

Susan
(alt. Susann, Suzan)
Hebrew, meaning 'lily'.

Susannah
(alt. Susana, Susanna, Susanne, Suzanna, Suzanne)
Hebrew, meaning 'lily'.

Svea
Swedish, meaning 'of the motherland'.

Svetlana
Russian, meaning 'star'.

Swanhild
Saxon, meaning 'battle swan'.

Sylvia
(alt. Silvia, Sylvie)
Latin, meaning 'from the forest'.

T Girls' names

Tabitha
(alt. Tabatha)
Aramaic, meaning 'gazelle'.

Tahira
Arabic, meaning 'virginal'.

Tai
Chinese, meaning 'big'.

Taima
(alt. Taina)
Native American, meaning 'peal of thunder'.

Tajsa
Polish, meaning 'princess'.

Talia
(alt. Tali)
Hebrew, meaning 'heaven's dew'.

Taliesin
Welsh, meaning 'shining brow'.

Talise
(alt. Talyse)
Native American, meaning 'lovely water'.

Talitha
Aramaic, meaning 'young girl'.

Tallulah
(alt. Taliyah)
Native American, meaning 'leaping water'.

Tamara
(alt. Tamera)
Hebrew, meaning 'palm tree'.

325

Famous artists

Barbara (Hepworth)
Bridget (Riley)
Louise (Bourgeois)
Tracey (Emin)
Yoko (Ono)

Tamatha
(alt. Tametha)

American, meaning 'dear Tammy'.

Tamika
(alt. Tameka)

American, meaning 'people'.

Tammy
(alt. Tami, Tammie)

Shortened form of Tamsin, meaning 'twin'.

Tamsin

Hebrew, meaning 'twin'.

Tanis

Spanish, meaning 'to make famous'.

Tanya
(alt. Tania, Tanya, Tonya)

Shortened form of Tatiana, meaning 'from the Tatius clan'.

Tao

Chinese, meaning 'like a peach'.

Tara
(alt. Tarah, Tera)

Irish Gaelic, meaning 'rocky hill'.

Tasha
(alt. Taisha, Tarsha)

Shortened form of Natasha, meaning 'Christmas'.

Tatiana
(alt. Tayana)

Russian, meaning 'from the Tatius clan'.

Tatum

English, meaning 'light hearted'.

Tawny
(alt. Tawanaa, Tawnee, Tawnya)

English, meaning 'golden brown'.

T

Taya

Greek, meaning 'poor one'.

Taylor

(alt. Tayler)

English, meaning 'tailor'.

Tea

Greek, meaning 'goddess'.

Teagan

(alt. Teague, Tegan)

Irish Gaelic, meaning 'poet'.

Teal

English, from the bird of the same name.

Tecla

Greek, meaning 'fame of God'.

Tehile

Hebrew, meaning 'song of praise'.

Temperance

English, meaning 'virtue'.

Tempest

French, meaning 'storm'.

Teresa

(alt. Terese, Tereza, Theresa, Therese)

Greek, meaning 'harvest'.

Terry

(alt. Teri, Terrie)

Shortened form of Teresa, meaning 'harvest'.

Tessa

(alt. Tess, Tessie)

Shortened form of Teresa, meaning 'harvest'.

Thais

Greek, from the mythological heroine of the same name.

Thalia

Greek, meaning 'blooming'.

Thandi

(alt. Thana)

Arabic, meaning 'thanksgiving'.

Thea

Greek, meaning 'goddess'.

Theda

German, meaning 'people'.

Thelma

Greek, meaning 'will'.

Theodora

Greek, meaning 'gift of God'.

Theodosia

Greek, meaning 'gift of God'.

Thisbe

Greek, from the mythological heroine of the same name.

Thomasina

(alt. Thomasin, Thomasine, Thomasyn)

Greek, meaning 'twin'.

Thora

Scandinavian, meaning 'Thor's struggle'.

Tia

(alt. Tiana)

Spanish, meaning 'aunt'.

Tiara

Latin, meaning 'jewelled headband'.

Tien

Vietnamese, meaning 'fairy child'.

Tierney

Irish Gaelic, meaning 'Lord'.

Tierra

(alt. Tiera)

Spanish, meaning 'land'.

Tiffany

(alt. Tiffani, Tiffanie)

Greek, meaning 'God's appearance'.

Tiggy

Shortened form of Tigris, meaning 'tiger'.

Tigris

Irish Gaelic, meaning 'tiger'.

Tilda

Shortened form of Matilda, meaning 'battle-mighty'.

Tillie

(alt. Tilly)

Shortened form of Matilda, meaning 'battle-mighty'.

Timothea

Greek, meaning 'honouring God'.

Tina
(alt. Teena, Tena)

Shortened form of Christina, meaning 'anointed Christian'.

Tirion

Welsh, meaning 'kind and gentle'.

Tirzah

Hebrew, meaning 'pleasantness'.

Titania

Greek, meaning 'giant'.

Toby
(alt. Tobi)

Hebrew, meaning 'God is good'.

Tomoko

Japanese, meaning 'intelligent'.

Toni
(alt. Tony)

Latin, meaning 'invaluable'.

Tonia
(alt. Tonja, Tonya)

Russian, meaning 'praiseworthy'.

Topaz

Latin, meaning 'golden gemstone'.

Tori
(alt. Tora)

Shortened form of Victoria, meaning 'victory'.

Tova
(alt. Tovah, Tove)

Hebrew, meaning 'good'.

Tracy
(alt. Tracey, Tracie)

Greek, meaning 'harvest'.

Treva

Welsh, meaning 'homestead'.

Tricia

Shortened form of Patricia, meaning 'aristocratic'.

Autumn names

Aeria
Axelle
Peace
Shanti
Zulma

Trilby

English, meaning 'vocal trills'.
Also a kind of hat.

Trina

(alt. Trena)

Greek, meaning 'pure'.

Trinity

Latin, meaning 'triad'.

Trisha

Shortened form of Patricia,
meaning 'noble'.

Trista

Latin, meaning 'sad'.

Trixie

Shortened form of Beatrix,
meaning 'bringer of gladness'.

Trudy

(alt. Tru, Trudie)

Shortened form of Gertrude,
meaning 'strength of a spear'.

Tullia

Spanish, meaning 'bound for
glory'.

Tunder

Hungarian, meaning 'fairy'.

Twyla

(alt. Twila)

American, meaning 'star'.

Tyler

English, meaning 'tiler'.

Tyra

Scandinavian, meaning 'Thor's
struggle'.

Tzipporah

Hebrew, meaning 'bird'.

Popular Scottish names

Alana
Catriona
Elsie
Elspeth
Flora
Heather
Isla
Kirsty
Morag
Rhona

T

U

Girls' names

Udaya
Indian, meaning 'dawn'.

Ula
(alt. Ulla)
Celtic, meaning 'gem of the sea'.

Ulrika
(alt. Urica)
German, meaning 'power of the wolf'.

Uma
Sanskrit, meaning 'flax'.

Una
Latin, meaning 'one'.

Undine
Latin, meaning 'little wave'.

Unice
Greek, meaning 'victorious'.

Unique
Latin, meaning 'only one'.

Unity
English, meaning 'oneness'.

Uriela

Hebrew, meaning 'God's light'.

Urja
(alt. Urjitha)

Indian, meaning 'energy'.

Ursula

Latin, meaning 'little female bear'.

Uta

German, meaning 'prospers in battle'.

Popular South American names

Adriel	Frances
Albany	Lily
Carolina	Mariana
Elena	Natalia
Eréndira	Poppy

Girls' names

Vada
German, meaning 'famous ruler'.

Valdis
(alt. Valdiss, Valdys, Valdyss)
Norse, meaning 'goddess of the dead', based on the mythological goddess of the same name.

Vale
Shortened form of Valencia, meaning 'strong and healthy'.

Valencia
(alt. Valancy, Valarece)
Latin, meaning 'strong and healthy'.

Valentina
Latin, meaning 'strong and healthy'.

Valentine
Latin, from the saint of the same name.

Valeria
Latin, meaning 'to be healthy and strong'.

Valerie
(alt. Valarie, Valery, Valorie)
Latin, meaning 'to be healthy and strong'.

Valia
(alt. Vallie)

Shortened form of Valerie, meaning 'to be healthy and strong'.

Vandana

Sanskrit, meaning 'worship'.

Vanessa
(alt. Vanesa)

English, from the *Gulliver's Travels* character of the same name.

Vanetta
(alt. Vanettah, Vaneta, Vanete, Vanity)

Greek, alternative of Vanessa, meaning 'like a butterfly'.

Vanity

Latin, meaning 'self-obsessed'.

Vashti

Persian, meaning 'beauty'.

Veda

Sanskrit, meaning 'knowledge and wisdom'.

Vega

Arabic, meaning 'falling vulture'.

Velda

German, meaning 'ruler'.

Vella

American, meaning 'beautiful'.

Velma

English, meaning 'determined protector'.

Venice
(alt. Venetia, Venita)

Latin, meaning 'city of canals'. From the city of the same name.

Venus

Latin, from the Roman goddess of the same name.

Vera
(alt. Verla, Verlie)

Slavic, meaning 'faith'.

Verda
(alt. Verdie)

Latin, meaning 'spring-like'.

Christmas names

Holly
Ivy
Mary
Natalie
Robyn

Verena
Latin, meaning 'true'.

Verity
Latin, meaning 'truth'.

Verna
(alt. Vernie)
Latin, meaning 'spring green'.

Verona
Latin, shortened form of Veronica. From the city of the same name.

Veronica
(alt. Verica, Veronique)
Latin, meaning 'true image'.

Veruca
Latin, meaning 'wart'.

Vesta
Latin, from the Roman goddess of the same name.

Vevina
Scottish, meaning 'pleasant lady'.

Vicenta
Latin, meaning 'prevailing'.

Vicky
(alt. Vicki, Vickie, Vikki, Vix)
Shortened form of Victoria, meaning 'victory'.

Victoria
Latin, meaning 'victory'.

Vida
Spanish, meaning 'life'.

Vidya
Sanskrit, meaning 'knowledge'.

Vienna
Latin, from the city of the same name.

Vigdis
Scandinavian, meaning 'war goddess'.

Vina
(alt. Vena)
Spanish, meaning 'vineyard'.

Viola
Latin, meaning 'violet'.

Violet
(alt. Violetta)
Latin, meaning 'purple'.

Virgie
Shortened form of Virginia, meaning 'maiden'.

Virginia
(alt. Virginie)
Latin, meaning 'maiden'.

Visara
Sanskrit, meaning 'celestial'.

Vita
Latin, meaning 'life'.

Vittoria
Variation of Victoria, meaning 'victory'.

Viva
Latin, meaning 'alive'.

Viveca
Scandinavian, meaning 'war fortress'.

Vivian
(alt. Vivien, Vivienne)
Latin, meaning 'lively'.

Vonda
Czech, meaning 'from the tribe of Vandals'.

Food and drinks-inspired names

Anise
Brandy
Cinnamon
Coco
Ginger
Madeleine
Olive
Polenta
Saffron

V

Girls' names

Waleska
Polish, meaning 'beautiful'.

Wallis
English, meaning 'from Wales'.

Walta
African, meaning 'like a shield'.

Wanda
(alt. Waneta, Wanita)
Slavic, meaning 'tribe of the vandals'.

Waneta
(alt. Wanita)
Variation of Wanda, meaning 'tribe of the vandals'.

Wanita
Variation of Wanda meaning 'tribe of the vandals'.

Wava
English, meaning 'way'.

Waverly
Old English, meaning 'meadow of aspens'.

Wendy
English, meaning 'friend'.

Wharton
English, meaning 'from the river'.

Whisper
English, meaning 'whisper'.

Whitley
Old English, meaning 'white meadow'.

Whitney
Old English, meaning 'white island'.

Wilda
German, meaning 'willow tree'.

Wilfreda
English, feminine form of Wilfred, meaning 'to will peace'.

Wilhelmina
German, meaning 'determined'.

Willene
(alt. Willia)
German, meaning 'helmet'.

Willow
English, from the tree of the same name.

Wilma
German, meaning 'protection'.

Winifred
Old English, meaning 'holy and blessed'.

Winnie
Shortened form of Winifred, meaning 'holy and blessed'.

Winona
(alt. Wynona)
Indian, meaning 'first born daughter'.

Winslow
English, meaning 'friend's hill'.

Winter
English, meaning 'winter'.

Wisteria
English, meaning 'flower'.

Wren
English, from the bird of the same name.

Wynda
Scottish, meaning 'of the narrow passage'.

Wynne
Welsh, meaning 'white'.

Bird names

Avis
Evelyn
Raven
Starling
Teal
Wren

 Girls' names

Xanadu
African, meaning 'of exotic paradise'.

Xanthe
(alt. Xanthe)
Greek, meaning 'blonde'.

Xanthippe
Greek, meaning 'nagging'.

Xaverie
Greek, meaning 'bright'.

Xaviera
Arabic, meaning 'bright'.

Xena
Greek, meaning 'foreigner'.

Xenia
Greek, meaning 'foreigner'.

Ximena
Greek, meaning 'listening'.

Xiomara
Spanish, meaning 'battle-ready'.

Xiu
Chinese, meaning 'elegant'.

Xochitl
Spanish, meaning 'flower'.

Xoey
Variant of Zoe, meaning 'life'.

Baby Names 2012

Xristina

Variation of Christina, meaning 'follower of Christ'.

Xylia

(alt. Xylina, Xyloma)

Greek, meaning 'from the woods'.

Popular Welsh names

Bronwen	Myfanwy
Carys/Cerys	Rhiannon
Elen	Sian
Guinevere	Tegan
Megan	Wynne

340

Girls' names

Yadira
Arabic, meaning 'worthy'.

Yael
Hebrew, meaning 'mountain goat'.

Yaffa
(alt. Yahaira, Yajaira)
Hebrew, meaning 'lovely'.

Yamilet
Arabic, meaning 'beautiful'.

Yana
Hebrew, meaning 'the Lord is gracious'.

Yanha
Arabic, meaning 'dovelike'.

Yanira
Hawaiian, meaning 'pretty'.

Yareli
Latin, meaning 'golden'.

Yaretzi
(alt. Yaritza)
Hawaiian, meaning 'forever beloved'.

Yasmin
(alt. Yasmeen, Yasmina)
Persian, meaning 'jasmine flower'.

Yelena
Greek, meaning 'bright and chosen'.

Yeraldina
Spanish, meaning 'ruled with a spear'.

Yesenia
Arabic, meaning 'flower'.

Yetta

English, from Henrietta, meaning 'ruler of the house'.

Yeva

Hebrew variant of Eve, meaning 'life'.

Ylva

Old Norse, meaning 'sea wolf'.

Yoki

(alt. Yoko)

Native American, meaning 'rain'.

Yolanda

(alt. Yolonda)

Spanish, meaning 'violet flower'.

Yoselin

English, meaning 'lovely'.

Yoshiko

Japanese, meaning 'good child'.

Yovela

Hebrew, meaning 'jubilee'.

Ysabel

English, meaning 'God's promise'.

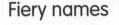

Fiery names

Ardea
Blaise
Enya
Vesta

Ysanne

Contraction of Isabel and Anne, meaning 'pledged to God' and 'grace'.

Yuki

Japanese, meaning 'lucky'.

Yuliana

Latin, meaning 'youthful'.

Yuridia

Russian, meaning 'farmer'.

Yusia

Arabic, meaning 'success'.

Yvette

(alt. Yvonne)

French, meaning 'yew'.

Z Girls' names

Zafira
Arabic, meaning 'successful'.

Zahara
(alt. Zahava, Zahra)
Arabic, meaning 'flowering and shining'.

Zaida
(alt. Zaide)
Arabic, meaning 'prosperous'.

Zalika
Swahili, meaning 'well born'.

Zaltana
Arabic, meaning 'high mountain'.

Zamia
Greek, meaning 'pine cone'.

Zaneta
(alt. Zanceta, Zanetah, Zanett, Zanetta)
Hebrew, meaning 'a gracious present from God'.

Zaniyah
Arabic, meaning 'lily'.

Zara
(alt. Zaria, Zariah, Zora)
Arabic, meaning 'radiance'.

Zelda
German, meaning 'dark battle'.

Zelia
(alt. Zella)
Scandinavian, meaning 'sunshine'.

Zelma

German, meaning 'helmet'.

Zemirah

Hebrew, meaning 'joyous melody'.

Zena

(alt. Zenia, Zina)

Greek, meaning 'hospitable'.

Zenaida

Greek, meaning 'the life of Zeus'.

Zenobia

Latin, meaning 'the life of Zeus'.

Zephyr

Greek, meaning 'the west wind'.

Zetta

Italian, meaning 'Z'.

Zia

Arabic, meaning 'light and splendour'.

Zinaida

Greek, meaning 'belonging to Zeus'.

Zinnia

Latin, meaning 'flower'.

Zipporah

Hebrew, meaning 'bird'.

Zita

(alt. Ziva)

Spanish, meaning 'little girl'.

Zoe

Greek, meaning 'life'.

Zoila

Greek, meaning 'life'.

Zoraida

Spanish, meaning 'captivating woman'.

Zorina

Slavic, meaning 'golden'.

Zosia

(alt. Zosima)

Greek, meaning 'wisdom'.

Zoya

Greek, meaning 'life'.

Zula

African, meaning 'brilliant'.